Over The Hill & On A Roll

BOB PHILLIPS
OVER 5 MILLION BOOKS SOLD!

HARVEST HOUSE PUBLISHERS
Eugene, Oregon 97402

OVER THE HILL & ON A ROLL

Copyright © 1998 by Bob Phillips
Published by Harvest House Publishers
Eugene, Oregon 97402

ISBN 0-7369-0002-0

Printed in the United States of America.

06 07 08 09 /BC/ 25 24 23 22 21 20

Contents

Over the Hill?
On a Roll?

During the 1970s, there was a very popular phrase among college young people: "Don't trust anyone over 30." Some people today think that 35 is middle age. Others believe that midlife crisis starts at 40. The question is, How can you tell if you're getting older? How can you tell if you're over the midway point of the hill of life? Here are some of the clues to this most difficult question.

The first clue is your belief that printers are using smaller type these days. You have to use a magnifying glass to read anything. On top of that, they're making print type so fuzzy that you have to hold it at arm's length to get it into focus.

Another clue is that people seem to be talking softer than they used to. You have to get people to keep repeating what they said, only a little louder. Many times you find yourself nodding your head in agreement with people even though you have no idea what they said.

You may be growing older if you think staircases are steeper these days and everything is farther than it used to be. Have you gotten to the point where you believe clothiers are making suits and dresses that shrink, shoelaces are harder to reach, snow is heavier, schoolkids are younger, food is more fattening, and other people your age are much older? That may be a clue.

Another way to tell if you've gone over the hill is a change of interests. Do you find yourself interested in early-bird specials and doggy bags? Have terms like arthritis, cellulite, crow's-feet, varicose veins, sunspots, and pacemakers entered your vocabulary? Have products like Poli-Grip, Geritol, Preparation H, Depends, and stewed prunes become household items?

When you begin noticing stretch marks, multiple chins, wrinkles, and folds—and your belt buckle is disappearing—it might be a sign that changes have occurred. A confirmation is when your upper arms hang and shake as you walk and your derriere drags on the ground.

When you put on your makeup with a trowel and your hair turns gray or even blue...you've probably gone over the hill. That is the time when you wish you could have some of Dick Clark's cells put into your body.

You can tell if you're over the hill when you put tenderizer in your oatmeal.

You can tell if you're over the hill when you get more get-well cards than junk mail.

You can tell if you're over the hill when your favorite exercise is a good brisk sit.

You can tell if you're over the hill when you begin using words like spry, plasma, salt-free, and fast temporary relief.

You can tell if you're over the hill when it takes a half-hour to wake up your leg.

You can tell if you're over the hill when you attend seminars on death planning, nutrition education, and grief therapy.

You can tell if you're over the hill when you believe that regularity is more important than popularity.

You can tell if you're over the hill when you talk to yourself and then complain of hearing voices. What you don't realize is that it's okay to talk to yourself, and it's okay to answer yourself. It's when you *disagree* with the answers that you've got a problem!

You're most likely over the hill if you can remember the following:

- When hardware used to refer to a store and not computer equipment.

- When "enter" was a sign on a door, not a button on a computer keyboard, and "chip" was a piece of wood.

- When fast food was what you ate during Lent, and it used to be that people married first and then lived together.

- When "rock music" took place while grandma sang a lullaby in a rocking chair, and kinky was for hair.

- When closets were for clothes and not coming out of, and aids were helpers in the principal's office or pills to help you when you were on a diet.

- When grass was for mowing, Coke was a refreshing drink, and pot was something you cooked in.

To write a book like *Over the Hill & on a Roll* is no easy task. It takes a great deal of persistence. In fact, I never knew the word "defeat"—along with thousands of other words I never knew the meaning of.

Actually, I come from a family of writers. My sister wrote books that no one would read. My brother wrote songs that no one would sing. My mother wrote plays that no one would see. And my father wrote checks that no one would cash.

When I first started writing, I contacted one publisher for encouragement and asked, "What is the best way to get started writing?" He said, "From left to right." I then showed him my material and said, "I've always wanted to be a writer in the worst way." He looked at my manuscript and said, "I think you've succeeded."

I knew that this man was unable to see true genius, so I mailed my manuscript to another publisher. Weeks went by and he never responded. Finally I got upset and sent him a letter asking him to read and publish my book immediately, or else return it, because I had other irons in the fire. My manuscript came back with a note that said, "I have read your book and advise you to put it with the other irons."

I decided to ignore the publishers' negative comments and sent copies of my manuscript to several other book editors. I got the following replies.

"Many thanks for your book; I shall lose no time in reading it." "Your book is fine. The only trouble is that the covers are too far apart." "Your book is out of this world, and I think that is the best place for it." "Your book is not to be lightly cast aside. It should be thrown with great force."

After being turned down by numerous publishers, I decided to write for posterity. I finally convinced a publisher to print some of my books. He took the risk and ended up publishing a number of my books. To date, the combined total of my books is over 5 million copies. If you don't believe it, come up to my house and count 'em.

In spite of all the encouragement I received, I decided to write another book anyway. I decided to get the last laugh by presenting to the world *Over the Hill & on a Roll*. I hope you have a fun time with it.

1

You're over the Hill When ...

You're over the hill when your feet hurt even before you get out of bed.

✦

You're over the hill when the rock stars you used to idolize are now potbellied and gray.

✦

You're over the hill when your gray hair isn't premature.

✦

You're over the hill when you try to straighten out the wrinkles in your socks and discover you're not wearing any.

—*Leonard L. Knott*

✦

You're over the hill when you realize how many people in power and authority are just winging it.

✛

You're over the hill when you think all of your friends are showing their age . . . but not you.

✛

You're over the hill when styles come back for the second time and you still have some left from the first time.

✛

You're over the hill when in the morning you stand and hear the usual snap, crackle, and pop, but it isn't breakfast cereal.

✛

You're over the hill when Medicare will pick up 80 percent of the cost of your honeymoon.

✛

You're over the hill when you don't go out at night because your back did.

✛

You're over the hill when your little brother starts going bald.

✛

You're over the hill when your mind tells you to stand on your own two feet and your body tells you to stay in the recliner chair.

✛

You're over the hill when your train of thought frequently derails.

✛

You're over the hill when you wake up looking like the picture on your driver's license.

✛

You're over the hill when you enter a store and totally forget what you came in for.

✛

You're over the hill when it takes you two tries to get up from the couch.

✛

You're over the hill when people stop saying you're looking good and start saying you're looking well.

✛

You're over the hill when instead of walking over and changing the channel, you spend 15 minutes looking for the remote.

✛

You're over the hill when Boy Scouts try to help you cross the street.

✛

You're over the hill when your idea of a night out is moving the TV out to the patio.

✛

You're over the hill when you talk about the good old days and nobody's qualified to call you a liar.

✛

You're over the hill when you fall asleep at the theater.

✛

You're over the hill when you refer to anyone under 40 as a kid.

✛

You're over the hill when they light your birthday candles and the automatic air-conditioning goes on.

✛

You're over the hill when by the time opportunity knocks, you have your hearing aid turned off.

✛

You're over the hill when you wait in line to take the escalator to the basement floor.

✛

You're over the hill when a senior citizen "swinging party" is where they spike the punch with Geritol.

✛

You're over the hill when the happy hour is a nap.

✛

You're over the hill when you start reading the ads for hemorrhoids, constipation, and hair loss remedies. Worse, you start buying the stuff.

✛

You're over the hill when all you can put your teeth into is a glass.

✛

You're over the hill when your arms aren't long enough to keep the newspaper in focus.

✛

You're over the hill when you're on vacation and your energy runs out before your money does.

✛

You're over the hill when old people are now elderly people.

✛

You're over the hill when you bend down to tie your shoelaces and you try to think of other things you ought to do while you're down there.

✛

You're over the hill when you can remember when children were strong enough to walk to school.

You're over the hill when you start buying those souvenirs you always wondered who bought.

You're over the hill when you can remember when Heinz had only one variety.

You're over the hill when your back goes out more than you do.

You're over the hill when your joints buckle and your buckles won't.

You're over the hill when you've seen five versions of The Adventures of Tom Sawyer at the movies.

You're over the hill when a telephone rings on the TV and you think it's yours.

You're over the hill when you open your outgoing mail.

✛

You're over the hill when bunnies are pesky, long-eared little animals in your garden.

✛

You're over the hill when the older you get, the farther you had to walk to school when you were a kid.

✛

You're over the hill when 90 percent of your dreams are reruns.

✛

You're over the hill when what you want for your birthday is a hot-water bottle.

✛

You're over the hill when heartburn is more frequent than heartache.

✛

You're over the hill when you know your way around but you don't feel like going.

✛

You're over the hill when you wear that comfortable sweater even though it has a hole in it.

✛

You're over the hill when you take a little nap before going to bed at night.

✛

You're over the hill when you can't remember if something was a dream or actually happened.

✛

You're over the hill when "burning the midnight oil" means staying up past 9 P.M.

✛

You're over the hill when your favorite night spot is a seat in front of the television.

✛

You're over the hill when everything starts to click: your elbows, knees, and neck.

✛

You're over the hill when you realize that you'll never live long enough to try all those recipes you've clipped from magazines.

✛

You're over the hill when you stop minding if someone else drives.

✛

You're over the hill when you decide procrastination is the best approach to life, but you never get around to it.

✛

You're over the hill when you say something for the first time that your father used to say and that you never liked.

✛

You're over the hill when you watch tabloid TV shows just to convince yourself how reprehensible they are.

✛

You're over the hill when mooning means romantic daydreaming.

✛

You're over the hill when you begin to realize that history textbooks include events you remember reading about in newspapers.

2

Name-the-Year
Quiz No. 1

Name the Year
192__

In the News
- Hitler dictates *Mein Kampf* from prison
- Aeroflot Soviet Airlines
- Teapot Dome scandal

New Products, Fads, and Fashion
- *Time* magazine
- Double-sided phonograph records
- Power windshield wipers
- The "Charleston"
- Waistlines lowered to hipbones
- Small hats curved down toward face

Music, Sports, and Entertainment
- Songs—"Yes, We Have No Bananas," "Charleston," "That Old Gang of Mine"
- Jack Dempsey retains heavyweight title
- Duke Ellington gets his start
- "The Happiness Boys"—radio
- Graham McNamee football broadcast—radio

Name the Year
193__

In the News
- March of Dimes
- Sulfa drugs
- "Wrong-way Corrigan" flies from New York to Dublin without permits
- "War of the Worlds" by Orson Wells disrupts nation

New Products, Fads, and Fashion
- Flexible drinking straws
- Barbershop quartets
- Bingo
- Knock-knock jokes
- Slinky gowns and bolero jackets
- Shirtwaist look

Music, Sports, and Entertainment
- Songs—"You Must Have Been a Beautiful Baby," "Jeepers Creepers," "Our Love Is Here to Stay"
- Eddie Arcaro rides first Derby winner
- Bob Feller strikes out 18 men
- Walt Disney's "Snow White and the Seven Dwarfs"
- "Information Please," "Pepsodent Show," "Life Can Be Beautiful"—radio

Name the Year
194__

In the News
- Selective Service System
- Boeing Stratoliner
- Wendell Willkie Challenges FDR

New Products, Fads, and Fashion
- Nylon stockings
- Waist-length outer jackets for men
- Playsuits—one-piece shorts and top

Music, Sports, and Entertainment
- Songs—"The Last Time I Saw Paris," "Tuxedo Junction," "When the Swallows Come Back to Capistrano"
- Count Basie, Les Brown, and Guy Lombardo become popular
- First color TV broadcast
- "Truth or Consequences," "The Quiz Kids," "Take It or Leave It," "Dr. Christian"—radio

Name The Year
195__

In the News
- Winston Churchill resigns as British prime minister
- President Eisenhower suffers massive heart attack
- Dr. Jonas Salk develops polio vaccine
- AFL and CIO become one single labor union

- Martin Luther King Jr. protests segregation
- Presbyterian Church ordains women ministers

New Products, Fads, and Fashion
- Ford Thunderbird
- McDonald's first restaurant
- Roll-on deodorants
- Filter cigarettes
- Big-money TV quiz shows
- The country goes Davy Crockett mad
- Pink shirts and flashy hatbands
- Tweed dirndl skirts and hooded sweaters

Music, Sports, and Entertainment
- Songs—"The Ballad of Davy Crockett," "The Yellow Rose of Texas," "Autumn Leaves," "Misty"
- Archie Moore knocks out Rocky Marciano
- James Dean is killed in sports car crash
- Elvis Presley (Elvis the Pelvis) is put under contract by RCA
- "The $64,000 Question," "Lawrence Welk," "Gunsmoke," "Captain Kangaroo," "The Mickey Mouse Club," "Father Knows Best," "The Honeymooners"—TV

Name the Year
196__

In the News
- The Peace Corps
- Green Berets special forces

- Berlin Wall is built
- Alan B. Shepard's suborbital flight
- National Council of Churches endorses birth control
- Tony Awards

New Products, Fads, and Fashion
- Pop top beverages
- Stereo FM radio
- LaPachanga dance step
- Kimono sleeves
- Sleeveless dresses
- Men's neckties are the narrowest

Music, Sports, and Entertainment
- Songs—"Moon River," "Roses Are Red, My Love," "Please, Mr. Postman," "The Exodus Song"
- Ernest Hemingway commits suicide
- Grandma Moses dies at age of 101
- "Ben Casey," "The Dick Van Dyke Show," "Car 54, Where Are You?"—TV*

---

* Quiz answers are located on p. 249.

3

Wisdom of the Ages

We grow old not so much by living but by losing interest in living.

From 30 to 45 runs the stage in which a man normally finds all his ideas—the first principles, at least—of that ideology which he is to make his own. After 45 he devotes himself to the full development of the inspirations he has had between 30 and 45.

—*Ortega Y. Gasset*

To say that a man is 30, 50, or 70 tells you very little more about him than if you were only told his name. The name, however, might convey nothing to you, whereas the age would induce you from force of habit to make an estimate of him which might prove entirely false.

—*Arthur Ponsonby*

✛

After a certain age, the more one becomes one-self, the more obvious one's family traits become.

—*Proust*

✛

I have often noticed that a kindly, placid good-humor is the companion of longevity, and, I suspect, frequently the leading cause of it.

—*Sir Walter Scott*

✛

No one frankly admits the foul offense of being nearer 60 than 50, but no one over 90 can resist boasting of it.

—*John Ayscough*

✛

To refuse to grow old is the unmistakable sign of youth.

✛

I find that a man is as old as his work. If his work keeps him moving forward, he will look forward with the work.

—*William Ernest Hocking*

✛

Nothing is more beautiful than cheerfulness in an old face.

—*Richter*

✛

When young we are faithful to individuals; when older we grow more loyal to situations and to types. When we meet such specimens, we seem to know all about them in an instant (which is true), and thus in spite of our decreasing charms we sweep them off their feet, for young people do not understand themselves and, fortunately for us, can still be hypnotized by those who do.

—*Cyril Connolly*

✛

After the age of 80, all contemporaries are friends.

—*Mme. De Dino*

✛

A person is always startled when he hears himself seriously called an old man for the first time.

—*Oliver Wendell Holmes, Sr.*

✢

People may grow old gracefully, but seldom gratefully.

✢

A person is not old as long as he is seeking something worthwhile.

✢

To avoid old age, keep taking on new thoughts and throwing off old habits.

✢

The most telling sign of old age is not caring anymore.

✢

Youth and beauty fade; character endures forever.

✢

You take all the experience and judgment of men over 50 out of the world and there wouldn't be enough left to run it.

—*Henry Ford*

✛

There is only so much time in the game of life. Between the ages of 50 and 60, I better attempt the other challenges because things change between 60 and 70.

—*Richard "Digger" Phelps*

✛

Everything I know I learned after I was 30.
—*George Clemenceau*

✛

From 40 to 50 a man must move upward, or the natural falling off in the vigor of life will carry him rapidly downward.

—*Oliver Wendell Holmes, Jr.*

✛

Grow up as soon as you can. It pays. The only time you really live fully is from 30 to 60.

—*Harvey Allen*

✛

Lord, Thou knowest better than I know myself that I am growing older. Keep me from getting too talkative, and thinking I must say something on every subject and on every occasion. Release me from craving to straighten out everybody's affairs. Teach me the glorious lesson that occasionally it is possible that I may be mistaken. Make me thoughtful, but not moody; helpful, but not bossy; for Thou knowest, Lord, that I want a few friends at the end.

✛

What's a man's age? He must hurry more, that's all; cram in a day what his youth took a year to hold.

—*Robert Browning*

✛

When you are young you want to change the world; when you are old you want to change the young.

✛

At 20 years of age, the will reigns; at 30, the wit; at 40, the judgment.

—*Benjamin Franklin*

✛

Almost all enduring success comes to people after they are 40. For seldom does mature judgment arrive before then.

—*Henry Ford*

✛

The young man is handsome, but the old superb.... Fire is seen in the eyes of the young, but it is light that we see in the old man's eyes.
—*Victor Hugo*

✛

Youth is a gift of nature; age is a work of art.

✛

Not by physical force, not by bodily swiftness and agility, are great things accomplished, but by deliberation, authority, and judgment—qualities with which old age is abundantly provided.

—*Cicero*

✛

Everyone is too old for something, but no one is too old for everything.

✛

No wise man ever wished to be younger.
—*Jonathan Swift*

✛

How old you really are depends on how many birthdays you're still looking forward to.

✝

The person who says he's too old to learn new things probably always was.

✝

I pity any person of 90 who reaches it with nothing more to show than how pleased he is to have reached it.

✝

As we grow older . . . we discover that the lives of most human beings are worthless except insofar as they contribute to the enrichment and emancipation of the spirit. . . . No one over 35 is worth meeting who has not something to teach us—something more than we could learn by ourselves, from a book.

—Cyril Connolly

✝

To see a young couple loving each other is no wonder; but to see an old couple loving each other is the best sight of all.

—William Makepeace Thackeray

✝

When we are old, we may sometimes enlighten, but we can no longer persuade.

—Madame Swetchine

✤

I believe that one has to be 70 before one is full of courage. The young are always halfhearted.

—*D.H. Lawrence*

✤

There are people whose watch stops at a certain hour and who remain permanently at that age.

—*Sainte-Beuve*

✤

The character we exhibit in the latter half of our life need not necessarily be, though it often is, our original character, developed further, dried up, exaggerated, or diminished: it can be its exact opposite, like a suit worn inside out.

—*Proust*

✤

To be 70 years young is sometimes more cheerful and hopeful than to be 40 years old.

✤

Perhaps one has to be very old before one learns how to be amused rather than shocked.

—*Pearl S. Buck*

✛

I promise to keep on living as though I expected to live forever. Nobody grows old by merely living a number of years. People grow old only by deserting their ideals. Years may wrinkle the skin, but to give up interest wrinkles the soul.

—*Douglas MacArthur*

✛

Old men dream dreams; young men see visions.

—*Melvin B. Tolson*

✛

Patience makes a woman beautiful in middle age.

✛

We grow neither better nor worse as we get old, but more like ourselves.

—*May Lamberton Becker*

✛

Nobody grows old by merely living a number of years. People grow old by deserting their ideals.

—*Samuel Ullman*

✛

We don't stop laughing because we grow old;
we grow old because we stop laughing.

✛

Nothing so dates a man as to decry the younger
generation.
—*Adlai E. Stevenson*

✛

Youth is not a time of life; it is a state of mind.

✛

It is possible that a person could live twice as
long if he didn't spend the first half of his life
acquiring habits that shorten the other half.

✛

When a man is young he writes songs; grown
up, he speaks in proverbs; in old age he
preaches pessimism.
—*Hebrew Proverb*

✛

The years between 18 and 22 were not given to
us to be frittered away in contemplation of
future tax shelters and mortgage payments....
Sometimes, of course, we lose sight of the heroic

dreams of youth later on, as overdue bills and carburetor problems take their toll. But those who never dream at all start to lose much more—their wit, empathy, perspective, and, for lack of a more secular term, their immortal souls.

—*Barbara Ehrenreich*

4

Bald Is Beautiful

I started going bald very early. In fact, in high school I was voted "Most Likely to Recede."

✝

Nothing makes a woman feel older than meeting a bald-headed man who was two grades back of her in school.

✝

They're just marketing a new cure for baldness. It doesn't grow hair—it just shrinks your head to fit what hair you've got left.

✝

Sometimes a man who does a lot of reflecting isn't bright; he's just bald.

✝

The most irritating fellow at most high school reunions is the man with only two things— money and hair.

✛

He washed his hair this morning and forgot where he put it.

✛

He keeps his hat on with a suction cup.

✛

My hair's getting thin, but then again, who wants fat hair?

✛

He's so bald that his head keeps slipping off the pillow when he sleeps.

✛

There are three ways that men can wear their hair: parted, unparted, and departed.

✛

Sure he's getting bald. People were certainly right when they said he'd come out on top.

✛

I won't even attempt to tell him a hair-raising story.

✛

I've been washing my hair too much—it's shrinking!

✛

He wears a wig. It makes him look at least ten years sillier.

✛

I'm not really bald. I've just got a tall face!

✛

The trouble with being bald is not so much in combing your hair as in knowing where to draw the line when you wash your face.

✛

People are always telling a woman how pretty her hair looks, but the only time they comment about a man's hair is when he no longer has any.

✛

Nature seems determined to make us work. The less hair we have, the more face we have to wash.

✛

People worry about their gray hair, but it's actually great to have gray hair. Ask any man who's bald.

✛

What a wife said about her bald-headed husband: I love to run my fingers through his hair because I can make better time on the open road.

✛

I was ahead of my time. I invented the dry look for men a long time ago. I went bald at an early age.

✛

There's one proverb that really depresses him: "Hair today, gone tomorrow."

✛

He has wavy hair . . . it's waving goodbye.

✛

There's one thing about baldness . . . it's neat.

✛

He's a man of polish . . . mostly around his head.

✛

He's so bald that it looks like his neck is blowing a bubble.

✛

He's so bald that he walks into a barbershop and asks for a shave and a shave.

✛

Today's toupees really fool people, but only those people who wear them.

✛

He has a beautiful head of skin.

✛

Hairdresser: Do you find split hair a problem?
Customer: Yes. Mine split a year ago!

✛

Old woman: Did you lose your hair by worrying?
Old man: Yes, worrying about losing my hair.

✛

At a certain time of life a man's hair begins to grow inward. If it strikes gray matter, it turns gray. If it doesn't strike anything, it disappears.

✛

A lot of people don't know this, but last week he quietly switched from Head & Shoulders to Mop & Glo.

✛

Consolation for Baldness

What's the advantage of hair, anyhow?
It blows in your eyes and it flops on your brow,
Disguising the shape of your scholarly head;
It often is gray and it sometimes is red.
Perhaps it is golden and ringleted, but
It needs to be combed and it has to be cut,
And even at best it is nothing to boast of,
Because it's what barbarous men
    have the most of;
Then challenge you, mirror, defiant
    and careless,
For lots of our handsomest people are hairless.
          —*Arthur Guiterman*

When you're losing your hair at the front, it means you're a great thinker. When you're losing your hair at the back, it means you're a great lover. But I'm losing mine at the front and the back. That means I think I'm a great lover!

5

Name-the-Year Quiz No. 2

Name the Year
192__

In the News
- Amelia Earhart becomes the first woman to fly the Atlantic
- Mickey Mouse makes his debut

New Products, Fads, and Fashion
- Safety glass
- Hardwater soap
- Potato chips
- The "Black Bottom" dance
- Pleated skirts
- Hair shingled
- Small hats

Music, Sports, and Entertainment
- Songs—"Button Up Your Overcoat," "Sweet Sue," "I Can't Give You Anything But Love"
- Ty Cobb retires
- Sonja Henie wins figure-skating title
- "National Farm and Home Hour," "The Voice of Firestone"—radio

Name the Year
193__

In the News
- FDR's "fireside chats"
- Japan occupies China north of the Great Wall
- Shantytowns occupy vacant lots
- Civilian Conservation Corps (CCC) hires young men
- Wiley Post becomes first person to fly solo around the world

New Products, Fads, and Fashion
- The term "G-men"
- Jigsaw puzzles
- Hair worn at shoulder-length
- Sandals become popular, along with open-toed pumps

Music, Sports, and Entertainment
- Songs—"Smoke Gets in Your Eyes," "Stormy Weather," "Easter Parade," "Inka Dinka Doo"
- Primo Carnera knocks out Jack Sharkey
- 80 million Americans go to the movies each week
- Disney's "Three Little Pigs" and "Who's Afraid of the Big Bad Wolf?" become popular
- "The Lone Ranger," "Helen Trent," "Ma Perkins"—radio

Name the Year
194__

In the News

- Atomic Energy Commission
- William Joyce (Lord Haw Haw) hanged for treason
- Baby Boom Starts

New Products, Fads, and Fashion

- Kaiser and Frazer cars
- Electric clothes dryers and electric blankets
- Automatic transmissions for cars
- Crew cuts
- Slim skirts below the knees
- Jackets with peplums and wide lapels

Music, Sports, and Entertainment

- Songs—"There's No Business Like Show Business," "Zip-a-Dee-Doo-Dah," "Shoofly Pie and Apple Pan Dowdy"
- Brooklyn and Cincinnati 19-inning scoreless baseball game
- W.C. Fields, who hated Christmas, dies on Christmas day
- "Talent Scouts," "My Friend Irma," "Harry James"—radio

Name the Year
195__

In the News
- Commonwealth of Puerto Rico
- Atomic-powered submarines—the Nautilus
- Potato shortage
- "I Like Ike" buttons
- Commercial jet flights
- Christine Jorgensen sex-change operation
- Revised Standard Version of the Bible

New Products, Fads, and Fashion
- Holiday Inns
- Uplifted or padded bosoms
- Bouffant skirts with crinoline petticoats
- Narrow neckties for men

Music, Sports, and Entertainment
- Songs—"Hi-Lili, Hi-Lo," "I Saw Mommy Kissing Santa Claus," "You Belong to Me"
- Rocky Marciano becomes heavyweight champion
- Dick Button wins both U.S. and Olympic figure-skating titles
- "Today Show," "The Guiding Light," "Jackie Gleason's Variety Show," "Adventures of Ozzie and Harriet," "I've Got a Secret," "This Is Your Life," "Dragnet"—TV

Name the Year
196__

In the News
- Flower children
- U.S. bombers attack Hanoi
- Great Britain legalizes homosexual behavior
- Christian Barnard performs first heart transplant
- Joseph Stalin's daughter, Svetlana Alliluyeva, moves to the U.S.
- Albert de Salvo, the "Boston Strangler," confesses

New Products, Fads, and Fashion
- Flashing colored lights at discos
- "Hippies"
- Ankle-length coats worn over miniskirts
- Paper dresses

Music, Sports, and Entertainment
- Songs—"Feelin' Groovy," "Michelle," "By the Time I Get to Phoenix," "Cabaret," "Sunrise, Sunset"
- Mickey Mantle hits his five-hundredth home run
- Cassius Clay loses heavyweight title for refusing military service
- Englebert Humperdinck begins to become known
- Joan Baez arrested at sit-in
- "The Lucy Show," "The Flying Nun," "The Smothers Brothers Comedy Hour"—TV

6

Midlife Crisis

Middle age is the time of life when a person starts declining almost everything.

✛

Middle age is when all you want for your birthday is not to be reminded of it.

✛

You are slightly past middle age if, before you step off the curb, you look down once more to make sure the street is still there.

✛

Middle age is the time of life when you can write a book about the things you talk yourself out of doing.

✛

Middle age has set in when a person starts making up excuses to do nothing.

✢

Middle age is when a narrow waist and a broad mind begin to change places.
                    —*Glenn Dorenbush*

✢

Middle age is when, instead of combing your hair, you start arranging it.
                    —*Herbert I. Kavet*

✢

An energetic middle life is, I think, the only safe precursor of a vitally happy old age.
                    —*Vida D. Scudder*

✢

A woman has reached middle age when her girdle pinches and the men don't.

✢

Middle age has arrived when a man's idea of get-up-and-go is to go to bed.

✢

Middle age is when the best exercise is one of discretion.
                    —*Lawrence J. Peter*

✛

Middle age is the time of life when a harrowing experience for a man is to listen to his wife brag about the big garden she wants.

✛

You've reached middle age when weight-lifting consists of just standing up.

✛

Middle age is the time of life when work begins to be a lot less fun and fun begins to be a lot more work.

✛

Middle age is when women stop worrying about becoming pregnant and men start worrying about looking like they are.

✛

Middle age is when you start out with your spirits up and end up with a rubdown.

✛

Middle age is the time of life when the hardest thing to raise in your garden is your knees.

✦

Middle age is the time of life when a man starts blaming the cleaners because his suits are shrinking.

✦

You're reaching middle age when it takes longer to rest than it did to get tired.

✦

The way I see it, you're only young once—and it takes years of middle age to get over it.

✦

Middle age is the time of life when the fellow who always acted like a human dynamo starts showing signs of ignition trouble.

✦

Middle age is when you hope nobody will invite you out next Saturday night.

✦

Childhood is the time when you make funny faces in the mirror. Middle age is the time when the mirror gets even.

✛

You can usually tell when you hit middle age:
It starts hitting back.

✛

A man reaches middle age as soon as he has to
throw his shoulders back to maintain his bal-
ance.

✛

Middle age is the time of life when a man con-
vinces himself that green lawn would look
better than a vegetable garden in his backyard.

✛

The hardest decision for a woman to make is
when to start middle age.

—*Warren Hull*

✛

Middle age is that period in life when your idea
of getting ahead is staying even.

—*Herbert V. Prochnow and
Herbert V. Prochnow Jr.*

✦

The really frightening thing about middle age is
the knowledge that you'll grow out of it.
—*Doris Day*

✦

A man reaches middle age when his waistline
clearly marks the halfway mark.

✦

Middle age is the time of life when a man starts
spreading in the middle and shedding on the
top.

✦

For most people, middle age is the time of life
when a man gets fat from having to eat all of
the brash conclusions he made in his youth.

✦

You're middle-aged if, when the air is springy,
you're not.

✦

Middle age has definitely arrived when your
wife suggests that you comb your hair differ-
ently so that it will look as though you have
more left than you really do.

✛

I wouldn't mind being called middle-aged if only I knew a few more hundred-year-old people.

—*Dean Martin*

✛

Middle age is when you suddenly find that your parents are old, your kids are grown up, and you haven't changed.

✛

Middle age is that span in life when you admit to no longer being young and deny being old.

✛

You've reached middle age when pulling your weight is a real drag.

✛

By the time most young men reach middle age they are more interested in saving their hair than they are in saving the world.

✛

Middle age is when you still believe you'll feel better in the morning.

—*Lawrence J. Peter*

✛

Middle age is that time of life when you finally know your way around but don't feel like going.

✛

Middle age is when your memory is shorter, your experience longer, your stamina lower, and your forehead higher.

✛

You've reached middle age when all you exercise is caution.

✛

Middle age is when you go all out and end up all in.

✛

An adult is a person who starts thinning on the top and thickening in the middle.

✛

Middle age is the time of life when a person knows how much work he should do, but manages to get by on half of it.

Middle age is when your wife tells you to pull in your stomach, and you already have.
—*Jack Barry*

Setting a good example for your children takes all the fun out of middle age.
—*William Feather*

A man knows he has passed middle age when his wife starts paying the premiums on his life-insurance policies long before they are even due.

7

Maturity

Our tastes change as we mature. Little girls like painted dolls and little boys like soldiers. When they grow up, the girls like the soldiers and the boys like the painted dolls.

Maturity is when you can sense your concern for others outweighing your concern for yourself.

At 16 I was stupid, confused, insecure, and indecisive. At 25 I was wise, self-confident, prepossessing, and assertive. At 45 I am stupid, confused, insecure, and indecisive. Who would have supposed that maturity is only a short break in adolescence?

—*Jules Feiffer*

I think age is a very high price to pay for maturity.

59

✛

The process of growing up is to be valued for
what we gain, not for what we lose.

✛

It costs a great deal to be reasonable; it costs
youth.

—*Madame de La Fayette*

✛

One stops being a child when one realizes that
telling one's trouble does not make it better.

—*Cesare Pavese*

✛

Maturity is the capacity to endure uncertainty.

—*John Finley*

✛

I believe that the sign of maturity is accepting
deferred gratification.

—*Peggy Cahn*

8

Name-the-Year Quiz No. 3

Name the Year
192__

In the News
- First meeting of League of Nations
- Mahatma Gandhi emerges

New Products, Fads, and Fashion
- Radio compass for aircraft navigation
- Rolls-Royce "Silver Ghost"
- First American submachine gun: "Tommy"
- Mah-Jongg
- Prohibition
- Model T closed sedan
- Elastic foundation garments
- White tennis shoes

Music, Sports, and Entertainment
- Songs—"Margie," "Avalon"
- Man O' War wins the Belmont and Preakness
- Agatha Christie's first publications
- Jazz becomes a worldwide rage

- Expressions—"belly laugh," "fall guy," "baloney," "sex appeal"
- Vaughn de Leath, "The First Lady of Radio"

Name the Year
193__

In the News
- Baseball Hall of Fame in Cooperstown, New York
- Chiang Kai-shek, Mao Tse-tung, and Chou En-lai unite to fight Japan
- The German dirigible Hindenburg bursts into flames while landing
- The Golden Gate Bridge spans San Francisco Bay

New Products, Fads, and Fashion
- Nylon
- Canasta becomes popular
- Inky Pinky rhyming riddles
- "Jitterbuggers"
- The Big Apple, the Shag, the Susie Q, and Trucking become the dance rage
- Shocking pink clothes
- Sloppy Joe Shetland wool sweaters
- Black-and-brown saddle shoes

Music, Sports, and Entertainment
- Songs—"In the Still of the Night," "Nice Work If You Can Get It," "Thanks for the Memories"
- Joe Louis knocks out James J. Braddock

- Joe DiMaggio becomes American League batting champion
- Benny Goodman is billed as "King of Swing"
- "First Nighter," "Chase and Sanborn Hour," "Edgar Bergen with Charlie McCarthy"—radio

Name the Year
194__

In the News
- American Broadcasting Company (ABC)
- The Pentagon
- Guadalcanal
- FBI switches from gangsters to spies
- Postal zoning

New Products, Fads, and Fashion
- *Esquire* magazine
- Streptomycin
- "Bobby soxers"
- Goldfish swallowing
- Prom dancing
- Bloomer playsuits
- "Zoot suit": single-button jackets, full-legged trousers, long chains, and broad-brimmed fedoras

Music, Sports, and Entertainment
- Songs—"People Will Say We're in Love," "Mairzy Doats," "Oh, What a Beautiful Mornin'"

- Leonard Bernstein of the New York Philharmonic
- Betty Grable is the new pinup rage
- "The $64,000 Question," "Take It or Leave It," "The Great Gildersleeve," "Here's Morgan"—radio
- Abbott and Costello, Jimmy Durante, Gary Moore—radio

Name the Year
195__

In the News
- American Football League
- U.S. compact cars
- Castro becomes Premier of Cuba
- Charles de Gaulle becomes President of France
- Nixon and Khrushchev argue in the "Kitchen Debate"
- Alaska and Hawaii admitted to Union
- Food stamp program for the poor
- Cranberry cancer scare

New Products, Fads, and Fashion
- Plastic garment covers used by dry cleaners
- Cardigan suits
- Lots of costume jewelry
- Wigs and wiglets

Music, Sports, and Entertainment
- Songs—"Mack the Knife," "The Battle of New Orleans," "He's Got the Whole World in His Hands," "Climb Ev'ry Mountain"
- Americans watch six hours of TV daily
- "The Untouchables," "Bonanza"—TV

Name the Year
196__

In the News
- Leonid Brezhnev replaces Nikita Khrushchev
- Pope visits the Holy Land
- Gulf of Tonkin attack
- Martin Luther King Jr. wins Nobel Peace Prize
- James Hoffa of the Teamsters Union found guilty

New Products, Fads, and Fashion
- Feature films on airplanes
- Touch-Tone phone dialing
- "Go-go" dancers
- Discotheques
- The Frug, the Swim, the Watusi, the Surf, and the Monkey become the popular dances
- The Beatles craze
- Short dresses and short white boots

Music, Sports, and Entertainment
- Songs—"Hello, Dolly," "Goin' Out of My Head," "Downtown," "I Want to Hold Your Hand"

- Cassius Clay becomes heavyweight boxing champ
- Beatles appear on Ed Sullivan's television program with long haircuts
- "Peyton Place," "That Was the Week That Was," "The Man from U.N.C.L.E."—TV

9
Smiles

When I was young there was no respect for the young, and now that I am old there is no respect for the old. I missed out coming and going.

—*J.B. Priestly*

✛

Everyone who's 50 swallows a little pride.

—*Jeannie Seely*

✛

I don't feel 80. In fact, I don't feel anything till noon. Then it's time for my nap.

—*Bob Hope*

✛

Patience is the ability to wait until you're too old to care anymore.

✛

What's become of the younger generation? They've grown up and started worrying about the younger generation.

—*Roger Allen*

✛

When you're young you just want to set the world on fire. Then you get older and just want to live close to the fire department.

✛

Why is it that at class reunions you feel younger than everyone else looks?

✛

The reason why some women over 50 have so many aches and pains is because they're over 60.

✛

A woman is as young as she feels like telling you she is.

✛

Fifty-five is the ideal age for a woman . . . especially if she is 65.

✛

It seems certain that fewer women would conceal their age if more men acted theirs.

✝

The reports of my death are greatly exaggerated.

—*Mark Twain*

✝

The worst thing about growing old is listening to your children's advice.

✝

One way to get silence at a woman's bridge club is to ask who is the oldest.

✝

The awkward age is when you are too old for the Peace Corps and too young for Social Security.

✝

When I was 18, I wanted to save the world. Now I'd be happy to save a hundred dollars.

—*Earl Wilson*

✝

By the time a man is wise enough to watch his step, he's too old to go anywhere.

—*Joey Adams*

✛

Old golfers never die. They just tee off and putt away.

✛

I was always taught to respect my elders, and I've now reached the age when I don't have to respect anybody.

—*George Burns*

✛

Wrinkles are hereditary. Parents get them from their children.

—*Doris Day*

✛

She was so old that when she went to school they didn't have history.

—*Rodney Dangerfield*

✛

A woman likes to be reminded about her birthday—but not which one it is.

✛

Except for an occasional heart attack I feel as young as I ever did.

—*Robert Benchley*

✦

Anyone can get old. All you have to do is live long enough.

—*Groucho Marx*

✦

One couple lived together for 60 years without a single argument. Their secret? They shared the same hearing aid!

✦

Age is a question of mind over matter. If you don't mind, it doesn't matter.

✦

At the age of 20 we don't care what the world thinks of us; at 30 we worry about what it is thinking of us; at 40 we discover that it wasn't thinking of us at all.

✦

When a man has a birthday he may take a day off. When a woman has a birthday she may take as much as five years off.

✤

Forty-five is said to be the prettiest age for women. But whoever heard of a woman that old!

✤

First you are young, then you are middle-aged, then you are old, then you are wonderful.

—*Lady Diana Cooper*

✤

When he said his right ear was warmer than his left ear, I knew his toupee was on crooked.

When you get to be my age, you go to the beach and turn a wonderful color: blue—from holding in your stomach!

✤

The first hint I got that I was getting older was when I played the slot machine and it came out three prunes.

I've found the secret of youth: I lie about my age.

—*Bob Hope*

✛

The trouble is that by the time you can read a girl like a book, your library card has expired.
                                        —*Milton Berle*

✛

Show me a wrinkle and I'll show you the nick of time.

✛

Nothing makes you resent birthdays like passing life's halfway mark.

✛

A woman's always younger than a man of equal years.
                          —*Elizabeth Barrett Browning*

✛

I always tell people I'm much older than I actually am—just to hear them tell me how good I look for my age.

✛

Things would be a lot nicer if antique people were valued as highly as antique furniture.

✛

A sure sign of old age is when you feel your corns more than your oats.

✛

By the time we get old enough not to care what anybody says about us, nobody says anything.

✛

The best way to tell a woman's age is when she is not around.

✛

Twenty years from now, the average age of the American girl will be five years older.

✛

Never ask a woman her age; ask it of some other woman.

✛

When a woman tells you her age, it's all right to look surprised, but don't scowl.

✛

I'll never make the mistake of being 70 again!

✛

The ten best years of a woman's life are between the ages of 29 and 30.

—*Peter Weiss*

✛

Whenever a man's friends begin to compliment him about looking young, he may be sure that they think he is growing old.

—*Washington Irving*

✛

I am an old man and have known a great many troubles, but most of them never happened.

—*Mark Twain*

✛

From birth to age 18, a girl needs good parents. From 18 to 35, she needs good looks. From 35 to 55, she needs a good personality. From 55 on, she needs good cash.

—*Sophie Tucker*

✛

Voltaire, asked for a consoling statement on the death of a man he disliked, wrote the following:

> "I have just been informed that Monsieur _____ is dead. He was a sturdy patriot, a gifted writer, a loyal friend, and

an affectionate husband and father—
provided he is really dead."

✛

Years ago we discovered the exact point, the
dead center of middle age. It occurs when you
are too young to take up golf and too old to rush
up to the net.

—*Franklin P. Adams*

✛

As long as a woman can look ten years younger
than her own daughter, she is perfectly satisfied.

—*Oscar Wilde*

✛

Fun is like life insurance: The older you get, the
more it costs.

—*Kin Hubbard*

✛

When women pass 30, they first forget their age;
when 40, they forget that they ever remembered
it.

—*Ninon de Lenclos*

✢

There is one thing about getting older: All the people you could have married now look like the one you did.

✢

As people become older they tend to become quiet. They have more to keep quiet about.

✢

I love it when people say, "You're not getting older, you're getting better," but I have one problem with that: The only thing I seem to be getting better at is getting older!

✢

An archaeologist is the best husband any woman can have: The older she gets, the more interested he is in her.

✢

The best place for a woman to hide her age is in the nearest beauty salon.

✢

A man who correctly guesses a woman's age may be smart, but he's not very bright.

✛

The best way to tell a woman's age is in a whisper.

✛

It's hard for the younger generation to understand Thoreau, who lived beside a pond but didn't own water skis and a snorkel.

—*Bill Vaughan*

✛

The young and the old have all the answers. Those in between are stuck with the questions.

—*Herbert V. Prochnow and Herbert V. Prochnow Jr.*

✛

It doesn't seem fair: By the time a person can afford to lose a golf ball, he can't hit it that far.

✛

You are only young once. After that you have to think up another excuse.

—*Billy Arthur*

✣

When I get up in the morning, the first thing I do is read the obituaries. If my name's not in there, I shave.

—*George Burns*

✣

Lack of pep is often mistaken for patience.
—*Kin Hubbard*

✣

After all, it isn't a crime to be 40. A pity maybe, but not a crime.

—*Jack Benny*

✣

Just when you've learned to make the most of your life, most of your life is gone.

✣

My older sister says she doesn't have wrinkles, she has laugh lines. She must do a lot more laughing at her age.

✣

Some women are very loyal. When they reach an age they like, say 35, they stick to it.

✢

When the census-taker asked how old she was, she couldn't remember whether she was 38 or 39, so she said 25.

✢

Many people are like the famous Liberty Bell—old, heavy, and slightly cracked.

✢

A woman rarely realizes her age until her birthday cake begins to look like a small forest fire.

By the time you learn all the lessons of life, you're too old and weak to walk to the head of the class.

✢

She wasn't old, but when she lit the candles on her birthday cake, six people passed out from heat exhaustion.

✢

The three ages of man are youth, middle age, and "My, but you're looking well!"

✛

A diplomat is a man who always remembers his wife's birthday but never remembers her age.
—*Robert Frost*

✛

By all means go ahead and mellow with age. Just be wary of getting rotten.

✛

By the time a man finds greener pastures, he's too old to climb the fence.

✛

I won't say he's old, but the picture on his driver's license is by Rembrandt.

✛

The trouble with life is that by the time a fellow gets to be an old hand at the game, he starts to lose his grip.

✛

I'm growing old by myself. My wife hasn't had a birthday in years.
—*Milton Berle*

His face is so wrinkled it can hold five days of rain!

✦

Then there was the woman who was cured of her nervousness in one treatment: The doctor told her it was a sign of old age.

✦

It's easy to find out how old a woman is: Ask her sister-in-law.

10

Old Age Happens

He's so old, his first job was parking covered wagons!

✛

You know you're getting old when all the names in your little black book are doctors.

✛

Old age is when you get that morning-after feeling without the night before.

✛

One of the nice things about old age is that you can whistle while you brush your teeth.

✛

He's so old he doesn't learn history—he remembers it.

✛

The only thing worse than growing old is to be denied the privilege.

✛

Old age is that period when a person is too old to take advice but young enough to give it.

✛

The best thing about getting old is that all those things you couldn't have when you were younger you no longer want.

✛

You can tell you're getting old when you sit in a rocking chair and can't get it going.

✛

Old age is the time of life when one learns what the statute of limitation is all about.

✛

Old age: when your memory is shorter and your stories are longer.

✛

Old age is that time of life when you spend more time talking to your pharmacist than anyone else.

✤

About the only thing that comes to us without effort is old age.

✤

Old age is when candlelit tables are no longer romantic because you can't read the menu.

✤

Old age: Just when you're successful enough to sleep late, you're so old you always wake up early.

✤

You know you're getting old when your toupee turns gray.

—*Milton Berle*

✤

You know you're getting old when the candles cost more than the cake.

—*Bob Hope*

✤

Most folks like the old days better—they were younger then.

✛

Old age is when you get out of the shower and you're glad the mirror is fogged up.

✛

He's so old that when he orders a three-minute egg, they ask for the money up front.
—*Milton Berle*

✛

Old age is always 15 years older than I am.
—*Bernard M. Baruch*

✛

I wouldn't say he's old, but I can tell you that his Social Security number is 2.

✛

We're as old as we feel, sad to say.

✛

Have you noticed that you have to get old before anybody will say you look young?

✛

A man is getting old as soon as he decides that it is a lot easier to run a lawnmower over the backyard than it is to plant a garden in it.

✣

A man is getting old when he encourages **a** woman to go out so that he can have the house to himself.

✣

You know you're getting old when getting lucky means you've found your car in the parking lot.

—*Bruce Lansky*

✣

Old age is ready to undertake tasks that youth shirked because they would take too long.

—*Somerset Maugham*

✣

Old age? That's the period of life when you buy a see-through nightgown and then remember you don't know anybody who can still see through one.

—*Bette Davis*

✣

You're aging when your actions creak louder than your words.

—*Milton Berle*

✛

The secret of longevity is deep breathing—as long as you can keep it up for 80 or 90 years.

✛

My uncle had the shortest will ever. It read, "Being of sound mind, I spent all my money."

✛

I'm not saying he's old, but his birthday cake has just been declared a fire hazard.

✛

Age is what makes furniture worth more and people worth less.

✛

What a married couple should save for their old age is each other.

✛

Age doesn't always bring wisdom. Sometimes age comes alone.

✛

Old age is when the gleam in your eyes is just the sun shining on your bifocals.

✛

One cannot help being old, but one can resist being aged.

—*Lord Samuel*

✛

As a person gets older he suspects that nature is plotting against him for the benefit of doctors and dentists.

✛

It takes about ten years to get used to how old you are.

✛

A gentleman in Georgia says he's at the age where he's too old for castor oil and too young for Geritol.

✛

He who is of a calm and happy nature will hardly feel the pressure of age, but to him who is of an opposite disposition youth and age are equally a burden.

—*Plato*

✛

Age has nothing to do with learning new ways to be stupid.

✛

Age does not depend upon years, but upon temperament and health. Some men are born old, and some never grow so.

—*Tryon Edwards*

✛

It's so sad that people are like plants—some go to seed with age and others go to pot.

✛

The woman who tells her age is either too young to have anything to lose or too old to have anything to gain.

✛

Age is strictly a case of mind over matter. If you don't mind, it doesn't matter.

—*Jack Benny*

✛

My husband is so old that he remembers Eve when she was just a rib.

11

Name-the-Year Quiz
No. 4

Name the Year
192__

In the News
- Amee Semple McPherson runs off with radio station operator
- Rudolph Valentino dies
- National Broadcasting Company (NBC)

New Products, Fads, and Fashion
- Book-of-the-Month Club
- The yo-yo
- 16-mm movie film
- Gum-chewing
- Above-the-knee skirts
- Cotton-waist dresses

Music, Sports, and Entertainment
- Gene Tunney defeats Jack Dempsey
- Babe Ruth called "The Sultan of Swat"
- Bing Crosby's first recording
- "Uncle Don" and his bedtime stories—radio

Name the Year
193__

In the News
- The Great Depression
- Albert Einstein arrives in U.S.
- Airline stewardesses

New Products, Fads, and Fashion
- Quick-frozen foods
- Photoflash bulbs
- Pinball machines
- Scotch tape
- Miniature golf
- Backgammon
- Hemlines below the knee
- Permanent-waved hair
- Longer hair with soft look

Music, Sports, and Entertainment
- Songs—"I Got Rhythm," Embraceable You," "On the Sunny Side of the Street"
- Bobby Jones wins golf's Grand Slam
- Louis Armstrong becomes popular
- Sinclair Lewis wins Nobel Peace Prize
- "Let's Pretend," "The American School of the Air"—radio
- Walter Winchell, Alexander Woollcott, Lowell Thomas

Name the Year
194__

In the News
- Department of Welfare and Education
- Ordinary people start to become psychoanalyzed
- Chiang Kai-shek and Nationalist goverment flee to Formosa (Taiwan)
- USSR explodes first atomic bomb

New Products, Fads, and Fashion
- Cortisone
- Minute Rice
- Pyramid clubs
- Canasta popular
- Full-circle felt skirts
- Mother-daughter dresses

Music, Sports, and Entertainment
- Songs—"Some Enchanted Evening," "Mule Train," "Younger than Springtime"
- Casey Stengel and New York Yankees win World Series
- Ezzard Charles defeats Joe Walcott
- Margaret Truman sings in Washington
- Arthur Miller's "Death of a Salesman"
- Dick Tracy and Tess Trueheart finally marry
- "Dragnet," "The Voice of Firestone,"—radio
- "Your Show of Shows," "Garroway at Large," "Kukla, Fran, and Ollie," "Captain Video,"—TV

Name the Year
195__

In the News

- Egypt seizes control of Suez Canal
- Fidel Castro leads uprising in Cuba
- Ringling Brothers and Barnum and Bailey Circus fold their tents forever

New Products, Fads, and Fashion

- Stereophonic sound
- Propeller beanies
- Tunic dresses and Turbans
- Men's Tyrolean hats

Music, Sports, and Entertainment

- Songs—"I Could Have Danced All Night," "Love Me Tender," "Que Sera, Sera"
- Floyd Patterson defeats Archie Moore
- Don Larsen pitches perfect game in World Series
- Babe Didrikson Zaharias dies
- Bobby Darin, Fabian, and Frankie Avalon become popular
- "Steve Allen Variety Show," "Tennessee Ernie Ford," "As the World Turns," "Leave It to Beaver"—TV

Name the Year
196__

In the News
- Gen. Aldolph Eichmann captured in Argentina
- Francis Gary Powers shot down in Soviet territory
- Contraceptive pills
- Heart pacemaker
- Laser beams
- Civil rights sit-in
- John F. Kennedy takes office

New Products, Fads, and Fashion
- Blue jeans shaped for female figure
- Bouffant hairdos
- Turtleneck sweaters
- Leather suits and coats
- Stretch pants

Music, Sports, and Entertainment
- Songs—"Never on Sunday," "Teen Angel," "The Twist," "We Shall Overcome"
- Rafer Johnson wins Olympic decathlon
- Wilt Chamberlain retires from basketball
- Floyd Patterson defeats Ingemar Johansson
- Bowling becomes popular
- NBC censors Jack Paar's joke on "Tonight Show"
- "Kraft Music Hall," "Flintstones," "Andy Griffith," "Nixon-Kennedy debates"—TV

12

Get in Shape

As you grow older you find it takes just about half as long to get tired and twice as long to get rested. The iron in your blood has turned to lead in the seat of your pants.

✛

Our vigor wanes with middle age: We find our footsteps lagging, our backbones creak, our sight grows dim, and yet our tongues keep wagging.

✛

Cosmetics were used in the Middle Ages; in fact, they're still used in the middle ages.

✛

The best way to stay young is to eat right, exercise, and lie about your age.

✛

Some people age well . . . and for others it's nip and tuck.

✛

Show me a man with his head held high and I'll show you a man who is having trouble adjusting his bifocals.

✛

If a woman of 50 is very thin, she can pass for years younger.

—*Audrey Hepburn*

✛

They say life begins at 40—but so do lumbago, bad eyesight, arthritis, and the habit of telling the same story three times to the same person.

✛

I've got to the age when I need my false teeth and my hearing aid before I can ask where I've left my glasses.

—*Stuart Turner*

✛

My doctor said I look like a million dollars— green and wrinkled.

—*Red Skelton*

✛

Forty is the age when you stop patting yourself on the back and begin doing so under the chin.

✛

You can tell you're getting older when everything hurts, and what doesn't hurt doesn't work.

✛

Time is a great healer, but it's no beauty specialist.

> —Herbert V. Prochnow and
> Herbert V. Prochnow Jr.

✛

It's hard to feel fit as a fiddle when you're shaped like a cello.

> —B. L.

✛

I'm not into working out. My philosophy: No pain, no pain.

> —Carol Leifer

✛

Diets are for persons who are thick and tired of it all.

✛

The 30-day diet is quite popular—that's the one people are going to start in about 30 days.

✛

If you're pushing 50, that's exercise enough.

✛

All a person has to do to become a millionaire in America is invent a low-calorie diet that tastes good to eat.

✛

The greatest time-saver I know is owning two pairs of eyeglasses.

✛

I'm at that age where I have nothing to do with natural foods; I need all the preservatives I can get.

✛

The three stages of getting sick: ill, pill, bill.

✛

She had her face lifted, but it turned out there was one just like it underneath.

✢

An adult is a person who has stopped growing at both ends and starts growing in the middle.

✢

An old bachelor in Kentucky finally fell in love. He got a cortisone shot so he could propose on bended knees.

✢

You know you're an adult when you've ceased to grow vertically but not horizontally.

✢

If I'd known I was going to live this long, I'd have taken better care of myself.

—*Jimmy Durante*

✢

I know she's got all her own teeth. I was with her when she bought them.

✢

You can only hold your stomach in for so many years.

—*Burt Reynolds*

✛

Some people grow up and spread cheer; others just grow up and spread.

✛

You can recognize the golden years by all the silver in your hair.

✛

Many of us are at the "metallic age"—gold in our teeth, silver in our hair, and lead in our pants.

✛

After 30, a body has a mind of its own.
—*Bette Midler*

✛

If only we could be old and sick while we're still young and healthy enough to put up with it!

✛

Life not only begins at 40—it begins to show.

✛

My diseases are an asthma and a dropsy and, what is less curable, 75.
—*Samuel Johnson*

✛

Cosmetics are used by teenage girls to make them look older sooner, and by their mothers to make them look younger longer.

✛

You are absolutely positive they build stairs steeper these days.

✛

I find it hard to make ends meet—ends like my fingers and toes.

✛

There are many people who seem to be broad-shouldered across the hips.

✛

Whatever Mother Nature gave me, Father Time is taking away.

✛

She's had her face lifted so many times it's out of focus.

✛

Nowadays there's a pill for everything—to keep your nose from running, to keep you regular, to keep your heart beating, to keep your hair from falling out, to improve your muscle tone. Why, thanks to advances in medical science, every day people are dying who never looked better.

13

You Know You're
Growing Old When . . .

You know you're growing old when you tried the seniors bowling league, but they all seemed a little immature.

✛

You know you're growing old when you always lose your train of thought somewhere between the subject and verb.

✛

You know you're growing old when the only thing you still do on the spur of the moment is sneeze.

✛

You know you're growing old when you've forgotten everybody's phone number, and most of their names, too.

✛

You know you're growing old when you still haven't started those 200 things you were going to do when you got time.

✛

You know you're growing old when the little old lady you help across the street is your wife.

✛

You know you're growing old when they don't print the large-print books large enough.

✛

You know you're growing old when it's much easier to see where you're going while driving if you straddle the dotted white line.

✛

You know you're growing old when your knees buckle but your belt won't.

✛

You know you're growing old when your children begin to look middle-aged.

You know you're growing old when nobody uses candles for your birthday anymore; they just set the whole cake on fire!

You know you're growing old when you lose your breath opening the telephone directory.

You know you're growing old when your mind is filled with great things to do, but your body vetoes every one of them.

You know you're growing old when you're finally able to resist temptation, but it doesn't come around much anymore.

You know you're growing old if you're pushing 60 and it's pushing back.

You know you're growing old when you paint the town red and have to take a long nap before you put on a second coat.

✛

You know you're growing old when your garage door opening has shrunk.

✛

You know you're growing old when you went shopping for a motorcycle and the whole store burst out laughing.

✛

You know you're growing old when you worked all those years, and now you can't remember what you did for a living.

✛

You know you're growing old when you remember when "hippie" meant big in the hips.

✛

You know you're growing old when you haven't seen the fourth quarter of a Monday night football game in five years.

✛

You know you're growing old when the 10 o'clock news is starting to come on later and later each night.

✦

You know you're growing old when your age is fast overtaking your heart rate.

✦

You know you're growing old when the loud music you used to complain about doesn't seem so loud anymore.

✦

You know you're growing old when your daily medications now come in 14 different colors.

✦

You know you're growing old when "hooked" was what Grandmother's rug might have been.

✦

You know you're growing old when you remember when radios plugged into the wall and toothbrushes didn't.

✦

You know you're growing old when a "trip" involved cars, planes, and ships.

✛

You know you're growing old when your medicine cabinet now holds more valuables than your bank account.

✛

You know you're growing old when sometimes you stop to think and forget to start again.

✛

You know you're growing old when you know what the moon looks like at 12:00, 2:00, and 4:00 A.M.

✛

You know you're growing old when "grass" was a ground cover, normally green.

✛

You know you're growing old when you can't imagine how you ever got along without a TV remote.

✛

You know you're growing old when you both go into the bedroom, dim the lights, and then can't remember why!

✛

You know you're growing old when you're just as pretty as you ever were, but now it takes an hour longer.

✛

You know you're growing old when you have trouble finding your kind of music on the radio.

✛

You know you're growing old when "roll" was a bun and "rock" was a stone.

✛

You know you're growing old when your most treasured household possession is your magnifying glass.

✛

You know you're growing old when you're keeping hundreds of cars behind you from breaking the speed laws.

✛

You know you're growing old when you don't go out as much as you used to because you can't remember why you used to.

✛

You know you're growing old when your name appears on every mail order list in the country.

✛

You know you're growing old when you get all upset because you can't find your glasses—and all you did was rest them on your forehead.

✛

You know you're growing old when the last place you and your spouse went together was the community health fair.

✛

You know you're growing old when you get huffy with the clerk in the store because he can't find the Metamucil!

✛

You know you're growing old when your bookshelf is overflowing with "How To" and "Self-Improvement" books but you've pretty well decided that you like yourself just the way you are.

✛

You know you're growing old when you use a silver rinse but your hair still comes out blue.

✛

You know you're growing old when you now need a computer to keep track of your daily medications.

✛

You know you're growing old when you figure you can fake it long enough to remain "computer-ignorant" the rest of your life.

✛

You know you're growing old when you burn the midnight oil after 8:00 P.M.

✛

You know you're growing old when you sink your teeth into a steak and they stay there.

✛

You know you're growing old when you eat oat bran every day, and it still doesn't help!

✛

You know you're growing old when you look around the market for a denture-flavored cereal.

✛

You know you're growing old when you've discovered that lately the newspaper is using smaller print.

✛

You know you're growing old when you ordered a steak the other night and were exhausted before you finished.

✛

You know you're growing old when people start telling you you're not getting older, you're getting better . . . and you believe them.

✛

You know you're growing old when you remember when a family went for a Sunday drive and everyone got in the same car.

✛

You know you're growing old when you use the stairs to get in and out of a swimming pool.

✛

You know you're growing old when there is more hair on your chest than on your head.

✛

You know you're growing old when some of your friends grow beards on their chins to camouflage the loss on the top part of their heads.

✛

You know you're growing old when they're making the golf balls heavier and putting the flags farther away.

✛

You know you're growing old when you now know more doctors than acquaintances.

✛

You know you're growing old when it takes you 16 blocks to reach the speed limit.

14

Name-the-Year Quiz No. 5

Name the Year
192__

In the News
- Lenin Dies
- Federal Bureau of Investigation (FBI)

New Products, Fads, and Fashion
- Kleenex facial tissue
- Crossword puzzles
- Maternity clothes
- Short hair for women
- Evening pajamas

Music, Sports, and Entertainment
- Knute Rockne of Notre Dame becomes popular
- Johnny Weissmuller wins Olympic honors—later becomes movie star in *Tarzan of the Apes*
- Republican National Convention—radio

Name the Year
193___

In the News

- Chiang Kai-shek declares war on Japan
- Drew Pearson's newspaper column
- Lindbergh baby kidnapper Bruno Hauptmann is electrocuted
- Boulder Dam forming Lake Mead is completed
- Queen Mary becomes largest ship afloat

New Products, Fads, and Fashion

- *Life* magazine
- "Gone with the Wind" craze
- Scavenger hunts become the rage
- Shoulders of women's dresses widened and padded
- Open-crown turbans

Music, Sports, and Entertainment

- Songs—"Pennies from Heaven," "I'm an Old Cowhand," "The Way You Look Tonight"
- Jesse Owens wins three Olympic events in Berlin—Adolf Hitler refuses to shake hands with him
- Joe Louis knocked out by Max Schmeling
- Count Basie begins to draw attention
- Zsa Zsa Gabor becomes Miss Hungary
- "Professor Quiz," "Columbia Workshop," "Stoopnagle and Bud" —radio

Name the Year
194__

In the News
- Mahatma Gandhi killed by assassin's bullet
- "Voice of America" broadcasts
- Test rocket missiles reaching speeds of 3000 mph
- Supersonic rocket planes
- Rear-engine Tucker automobile

New Products, Fads, and Fashion
- Long-playing phonograph records
- Fitted bed sheets
- Velcro
- Skirts shorter
- Waistlines less pinched

Music, Sports, and Entertainment
- Songs—"Buttons and Bows," "On a Slow Boat to China," "All I Want for Christmas Is My Two Front Teeth"
- Citation becomes horse of the year
- Bob Mathias wins decathlon at summer Olympics
- Dick Button wins gold medal for men's figure skating
- Milton Berle becomes TV star
- Four TV networks—CBS, NBC, ABC, and Dumont Television
- "Stop the Music," "Duffy's Tavern," Louella Parsons, Jimmy Fidler—radio

- "The Texaco Star Theatre," "Hopalong Cassidy," "Ford Theater," "Toast of the Town," "Break the Bank"—TV

Name the Year
195__

In the News
- National Council of Churches
- War between North and South Korea begins
- Elizabeth Taylor marries for first time

New Products, Fads, and Fashion
- Antihistamines
- Diner's Club credit cards
- Xerox copying
- Orlon
- Layered look with mix-and-match separates

Music, Sports, and Entertainment
- Songs—"From This Moment On," "Tennessee Waltz," "I've Never Been in Love Before"
- Joe Louis attempts comeback and fails to Ezzard Charles
- President Truman strikes out at music critic Paul Hume for criticizing Margaret Truman's singing
- "The Big Show" with Tallulah Bankhead, "Steve Allen Show," "Grand Central Station"—radio
- "The Lucky Strike Hit Parade," "You Bet Your Life," "The Colgate Comedy Hour"—TV

Name the Year
196__

In the News
- Boeing 747 carries up to 500 passengers
- Cyclamates and artificial sweeteners removed from the market
- Man walks on the moon
- Golda Meir becomes prime minister of Israel
- The "Chicago Eight" indicted
- William L. Calley stands trial for premeditated murder of South Vietnamese civilians at My Lai
- Charles Manson indicted for the murder of Sharon Tate

New Products, Fads, and Fashion
- Disposable diapers
- Occult for the average man becomes popular
- Velvet suits and ruffled shirts

Music, Sports, and Entertainment
- Songs—"Aquarius," "Raindrops Keep Falling on My Head," "I'll Never Fall in Love Again," "Didn't We," "A Time for Us"
- New York Mets take the National League and World Series
- Rod Laver wins at Wimbledon and Forest Hills
- Tiny Tim ("Tip-Toe Through the Tulips") marries Miss Vicki live on Johnny Carson's "Tonight Show"
- "The Bold Ones," "Hawaii Five-O"—TV

15

Memory Madness

There's an advantage in having a poor memory:
You have less to forget.

✢

I don't let old age bother me. There are three
signs of old age: Loss of memory . . . I forget the
other two.

—*Red Skelton*

When I was younger I could remember anything, whether it had happened or not.

—*Mark Twain*

✢

The advantage of a bad memory is that one
enjoys several times the same good things for
the first time.

—*Friedrich Nietzsche*

✢

Memory is the thing I forget with.

✣

I have a photographic memory, but sometimes I forget to take off the lens cap.

✣

Youth longs and manhood strives, but age remembers.
                                    —*Oliver Wendell Holmes Sr.*

✣

How cruelly sweet are the echoes that start when memory plays an old tune on the heart.
                                    —*Cook*

✣

If you don't think people have good memories, try repeating a joke you told them about a month ago.

✣

Memory is a faculty that reminds you that you've probably forgotten something.

✣

The reason people can remember the "good old days" is that there were so few of them.

✛

We can remember minutely and precisely only
the things which never really happened to us.
                                    —*Eric Hoffer*

✛

Anybody who tells you he never made a mistake in his life is probably relying on a poor
memory—his or yours.

✛

There is no point in worrying about forgetting
things as you grow older because you'll soon
forget what you forgot.

✛

Nostalgia is remembering the pleasures of sitting in front of a big fireplace—without remembering you had to cut the wood for it.

✛

Nothing improves the memory more than
trying to forget.

✛

You must arrange in advance for pleasant
memories.

✛

Nothing is more responsible for the "good old days" than a poor memory.

✛

A retentive memory is a good thing, but the ability to forget is the true token of greatness.
—*Elbert Hubbard*

✛

Recollection is the only paradise from which we cannot be turned out.
—*Jean Paul Richter*

✛

Most people would rather look backward than forward because it's easier to remember where you've been than to figure out where you're going.

✛

Memory is a wonderful treasure chest for those who know how to pack it.

✛

There are three kinds of memory—good, bad, and convenient.

✛

There's nothing a person can do to improve himself so much as writing his memoirs.

✛

When saving for old age, be sure to lay up a few pleasant thoughts.

✛

Why can we remember the tiniest detail that has happened to us, and not remember how many times we have told it to the same persons?
—*Francois de La Rochefoucauld*

✛

Let us not burden our remembrances with a heaviness that is gone.
—*William Shakespeare*

✛

You never realize what a good memory you have until you try to forget something.

✛

He who is not very strong in memory should not meddle with lying.
—*Michel de Montaigne*

✦

Everyone complains about his memory, and no one complains about his judgment.
—*Francois de La Rochefoucauld*

✦

Memory is the cabinet of imagination, the treasury of reason, the registry of conscience, and the council chamber of thought.
—*St. Basil*

✦

One way to improve your memory is to lend people money.

✦

Nothing is more common than a fool with a strong memory.
—*C.C. Colton*

✦

A wise man once told me that the best thing about memories is that you can remember them without having to relive them.

✦

Of all liars, the smoothest and most convincing is the memory.

✙

Memory is a diary that chronicles things that never have happened, and couldn't possibly have happened.

—*Oscar Wilde*

✙

That which is bitter to endure may be sweet to remember.

—*Thomas Fuller*

✙

There is a wicked inclination in most people to suppose an old man decayed in his intellect. If a young or middle-aged man, when leaving a company, does not recollect where he laid his hat, it is nothing; but if the same inattention is discovered in an old man, people will shrug up their shoulders and say, "His memory is going."

—*Samuel Johnson*

✙

I never heard of an old man forgetting where he buried his money.

—*Cicero*

✙

I have a memory like an elephant. In fact, elephants often consult me.

—*Noel Coward*

✛

I had a terrible experience last week. I enrolled for a memory course and forgot why.

✛

Not the power to remember, but its very opposite, the power to forget, is a necessary condition for our existence.

—*Sholem Asch*

✛

What was hard to endure is sweet to recall. Good memories have ill judgments.

✛

Memory of happiness makes misery woeful.

✛

The true art of memory is the art of attention.

✛

How sweet to remember the trouble that is past!

✛

In plucking the fruit of memory one runs the risk of spoiling its bloom.

—*Joseph Conrad*

✛

Writing things down is the best secret of a good memory.

✛

Sorrow remembered sweetens present joy.

✛

The right honorable gentleman is indebted to his memory for his jests and to his imagination for his facts.

—R.B. Sheridan

✛

"The horror of that moment," the King went on, "I shall never, never forget!"

"You will, though," the Queen said, "if you don't make a memorandum of it."

—Lewis Carroll

✛

I could never remember names until I took that great Sam Carnegie course.

16

Middle-Age Crazies

Middle age is the time of life when you wonder how you could have been stupid enough to organize a picnic for a group of ten-year-olds.

✢

One of the many things nobody ever tells you about middle age is that it's such a nice change from being young.

—*Dorothy Canfield Fisher*

✢

Middle age is having a choice of two temptations and choosing the one that will get you home earlier.

—*Dan Bennett*

✢

Whoever, in middle age, attempts to realize the wishes and hopes of his early youth invariably deceives himself. Each ten years of a man's life has its own fortunes, its own hopes, its own desires.

—*Goethe*

✛

You've reached middle age when people begin to recognize you from the rear, too.

✛

A sure sign of middle age is the size of the obstacle that gets in your way when you tie your shoes.

✛

Middle age is when your clothes no longer fit, and it's not the clothes that need the alterations.

✛

Middle age is when a man is always thinking that in a week or two he will feel as good as ever.

—*Don Marquis*

✛

Middle age is when you begin to exchange your emotions for symptoms.

—*Irvin S. Cobb*

✛

A middle-aged man's idea of a roaring good time is to enjoy it all from a sitting position.

✛

Middle age is when all one's energy goes to waist.

✛

A middle-aged man's waistline is his line of least resistance.

✛

You're middle-aged when your stomach goes out for a career of its own.

✛

A woman is at middle age when she takes her high school annual out of the bookcase and hides it where the children can't find it.

✛

Middle age has set in when a man is more interested in what his wife's clothes cost than in how they fit her.

✛

A woman reaches middle age when she is willing to wear shoes that fit her comfortably.

✛

Middle age is when you're willing to get up and
give your seat to a lady—and can't.

—*Sammy Kaye*

✛

You're middle-aged when your idea of
unwinding on a Friday night is to go to bed and
read.

✛

When a middle-aged man says he's worried
about fallout, he probably means hair, not
atoms.

✛

Middle age is when you've met so many people
that every new person you meet reminds you of
someone else.

—*Ogden Nash*

✛

In middle age you are as young as ever but it
takes a lot more effort.

✛

Nothing stumps a middle-aged man like trying
to get into last summer's bathing suit.

✛

Middle age is when you've given up all your bad habits and still don't feel good.

✛

By the time we're ready to admit we've reached middle age, we're beyond it.

✛

The least likely way for a middle-aged woman to celebrate her birthday is annually.

✛

Middle age is when a woman's hair starts turning from gray to black.

✛

Modern medicine still hasn't decided whether it's harder on a middle-aged man to mow the lawn himself or argue to get his teenage son to do it.

✛

A man has reached middle age when all it takes to get him exhausted is a little bit of child's play.

✦

The gift from middle age was the ability to
enjoy the moment without expecting it to last.
—*Lisa Alther*

✦

Middle age is when we can do just as much as
ever but would rather not.
—*Laurence J. Peter*

✦

Middle age has already arrived when the
thought of doing weight-lifting exercises is
enough to exhaust you.

✦

There are two ways to determine middle age;
one is by the calendar, and the other by the
waistline.

✦

Youth looks ahead, old age looks back, and
middle age looks tired.

✦

Middle age is the time of life when most men
find it much harder to throw their weight
around . . . or away.

✛

One thing is certain about middle age: You wonder how you got there so fast.

✛

When you begin to smile at things that once caused you to laugh, middle age is approaching.

✛

Middle age is the time of life when a man who used to go like 60 now has to push himself just to go like 30.

✛

Middle age is when you start eating what's good for you instead of what you like.

✛

The five B's of middle age are: baldness, bridgework, bifocals, bay windows, and bunions.

✛

Middle age is when a man finds he's taking his teeth out more than he takes his wife out.

✢

Middle age is the time of life when you're lucky if you can reach the phone before it rings three times.

✢

One of the chief pleasures of middle age is looking back at the people you didn't marry.

✢

Middle age is the time of life when the price you pay for a little fun goes up each time.

✢

When a man turns off the light for economical reasons rather than for romantic reasons, he has definitely reached middle age.

✢

Middle age is when you know all the answers, but no one asks the questions.

✢

One way a man can tell whether or not he's reached middle age is to babysit for his first grandchild.

✜

You've reached middle age when a lot of living under your belt begins to show there.

✜

Middle age is when you stop criticizing the older generation and start criticizing the younger one.

✜

Middle age is when you look into the mirror and wish you hadn't.

✜

Middle age is when you are sitting at home on a Saturday night and the telephone rings and you hope it isn't for you.

—*Ogden Nash*

✜

Middle age is the time of life when a man becomes determined to diet each time he buys a new suit.

✜

Middle age is actually the prime of life—it just takes a little longer to get primed.

17

Name-the-Year Quiz
No. 6

Name the Year
192__

In the News
- Leon Trotsky kicked out of USSR
- Graf Zeppelin completes around-the-world trip
- Stock market crash begins
- Seeing Eye Foundation
- Columbia Broadcasting System (CBS)

New Products, Fads, and Fashion
- Cosmetics abound
- Bridge playing
- Hemlines short
- Fake pearl necklaces

Music, Sports, and Entertainment
- Songs—"Ain't Misbehavin'," "Singin' in the Rain," "Happy Days Are Here Again"
- Connie Mack is honored for service to his city
- 618 radio stations
- H. V. Kaltenborne news commentator—radio

- "Amos 'n' Andy"—radio
- Kate Smith, Rudy Vallee, Arthur Godfrey—radio

Name the Year
193__

In the News
- The Star Spangled Banner becomes official national anthem
- The "Tin Goose"—Ford Tri-Motor airplane
- Gangster Al Capone charged with income tax evasion
- 1300 banks close
- Empire State Building (with 102 stories) opens

New Products, Fads, and Fashion
- Electric dry shaver
- Electron microscope
- Baggy knickers and wool socks
- Saddle shoes
- Soft shirts

Music, Sports, and Entertainment
- Songs—"Goodnight, Sweetheart," "Dancing in the Dark," "I Found a Million-Dollar Baby in the Five-and-Ten-Cent Store"
- Knute Rockne killed in plane crash
- Kate Smith sings "When the Moon Comes over the Mountain"
- Milton Berle becomes a vaudeville hit

- "The March of Time," "Little Orphan Annie," "Lum and Abner"—radio

Name the Year
194__

In the News
- The World Bank
- G.I. Bill of Rights
- German V-2 rocket
- RAF bombs Berlin
- Normandy invasion
- Battle of the Bulge
- FDR defeats Dewey to serve fourth term as President
- Ringling Brothers and Barnum and Bailey Circus fire

New Products, Fads, and Fashion
- "Kilroy Was Here"
- "Gobbledygook" a new word
- Cartoon characters "Willie and Joe" and "Private Sad Sack"
- Rayon blouses and hose
- Jeans with white shirts hanging out

Music, Sports, and Entertainment
- Songs—"Rum and Coca-Cola," "Don't Fence Me In," "Swinging on a Star"
- Glenn Miller is killed while playing for armed forces

- "The Man Behind the Gun," "FBI in Peace and War," "Nick Carter," "The Life of Riley"—radio

Name the Year
195__

In the News
- National Aeronautics and Space Agency (NASA)
- American Association of Retired Persons
- Khrushchev replaces Bulganin and becomes head of government and Communist Party

New Products, Fads, and Fashion
- Trading stamps in supermarkets
- Bank of America credit cards
- Trapeze silhouette dresses—tentlike shape
- Mohair sweaters

Music, Sports, and Entertainment
- Songs—"The Chipmunk Song," "Thank Heaven for Little Girls," "The Purple People Eater," "Tom Dooley"
- Althea Gibson breaks color lines and wins at Wimbledon
- Eddie Arcaro celebrates his four-thousandth win
- Van Cliburn becomes famous overnight
- "Doctor Zhivago" becomes popular worldwide
- "Twenty-One," "77 Sunset Strip"—TV

Name the Year
196__

In the News
- Telstar I launched by NASA
- U.S. military assistance given to South Vietnam
- John Glenn orbits the earth
- Marilyn Monroe dies from barbiturate overdose
- Full integration in U.S. military reserve

New Products, Fads, and Fashion
- The bossa nova dance
- Wigs become popular
- A-line dresses
- Pillbox hats

Music, Sports, and Entertainment
- Songs—"Ramblin Rose," "Return to Sender," "Go Away, Little Girl," "A Taste of Honey," "Breaking Up Is Hard to Do"
- Sonny Liston knocks out Floyd Patterson
- The first Beatles record
- Johnny Carson hosts "The Tonight Show"
- Jacqueline Kennedy takes country on color TV tour of the White House
- "The Virginian," "The Beverly Hillbillies," "Roy Rogers/Dale Evans Variety Hour"—TV

18

Grandparents

Grandchildren of any age can always make their grandparents happy just by saying, "I'm hungry!"

✛

They say grandchildren brighten up the home. That's right—they never turn off the lights.

✛

Among the things that are quite easy, even simple, for a child to operate are the grandparents.

✛

A little boy wrote this letter to his grandmother: "Dear Grandmother, I'm very sorry that I forgot your birthday last week. It would serve me right if you forgot mine next Tuesday."

✛

Grandfather on airplane: Have I told you about my grandchildren?

Occupant in the next seat: No, and I certainly
do appreciate it!

✣

A five-year-old girl had gone fishing with her
grandfather. After an hour or so her grandfather asked her, "Are you having any luck?"

She replied indignantly, "No, I don't think my
worm is really trying."

✣

All it takes for the average woman to discover
her second wind is to become a grandmother.

✣

The ones who usually manage to get the most
out of middle age are the grandchildren.

✣

Nothing adds to the popularity of a grandparent around the house like an unexpected
need for a reliable babysitter.

✣

Grandparents can contribute a lot to a young
man's success, especially if they're very
wealthy.

✤

There is no better medicine for ailing grand-parents than baby grandchildren.

✤

Almost every grandparent will tell you that spanking is unnecessary for your children, even though they felt it was necessary for you.

✤

One of the greatest pleasures a person can experience is to gaze upon grandchildren when they're fast asleep.

✤

Our younger generation is quite safe as long as they have grandparents to protect them.

✤

Perfect love sometimes does not come until the first grandchild.

✤

Nothing makes a boy smarter than being a grandson.

✤

Little boy: Grandpa, were you on the ark?

Grandpa: Of course not!
Little boy: Then how come you weren't drowned?

Over the river and through the wood,
To grandmother's house we'll go;
The horse knows the way
To carry the sleigh
Through the white and drifted snow.
—*Lydia Maria Child*

Traffic sign in Florida mobile-home park: Slow, Grandparents at play.

Grandchildren are God's rewards to grandparents for not shooting their children.

Just about the time a woman thinks her work is done, she becomes a grandmother.

Some of our modern grandmothers are so young and spry they help the Boy Scouts across the street.

✛

Nothing is harder on a grandparent than having to watch a grandchild be disciplined.

✛

Grandparents are people who come to your house, spoil the children, and then go home.

✛

No cowboy was ever faster on the draw than a grandparent pulling a baby picture out of a wallet.

✛

The commonest axiom of history is that every generation revolts against its fathers and makes friends with its grandfathers.
—*Lewis Mumford*

✛

Someone said a child is a person who is frequently spoiled because you can't spank the two grandmothers.

✛

There are fathers who do not love their children; there is no grandfather who does not adore his grandson.
—*Victor Hugo*

✢

A man begins to show his age at about the same time he begins to show pictures of his grandchildren.

✢

Grandchildren don't make a man feel old—it's knowing that he's married to a grandmother.

✢

Child's definition of grandmother: that white-haired lady who keeps mommy from spanking me.

✢

Grandpa and grandma were too busy scratching for a living to need books on how to stop worrying.

✢

A grandmother is a babysitter who watches the kids instead of the television.

✢

If becoming a grandmother was only a matter of choice I should advise every one of you straightway to become one. There is no fun for old people like it!

—*Hannah Smith*

✛

The closest friends I have made all through life have been people who also grew up close to a loved and loving grandmother or grandfather.

—*Margaret Mead*

✛

Grandparents are frequently more congenial with their grandchildren than with their children. An old man, having retired from active life, regains the gaiety and irresponsibility of childhood. He is ready to play. . . . He cannot run with his son, but he can totter with his grandson. Our first and last steps have the same rhythm; our first and last walks are similarly limited.

—*André Maurois*

✛

Our children are here to stay, but our babies and toddlers and preschoolers are gone as fast as they grow up, and we have only a short moment with each. When you see a grandfather take a baby in his arms, you see that the moment hasn't always been long enough.

—*St. Clair Adams Sullivan*

19

Old-Timers

An old-timer is someone who can remember when going to the eternal rest didn't mean landing a job with the government.

An old-timer is someone who remembers when children didn't ask what a cow was; they were told to get up at dawn and go milk one.

You're an old-timer if you can remember when just about the only labor-saving device was Sunday.

An old-timer is the married man who can remember when the only guided missiles were small vases and rolling pins.

You're an old-timer if you can remember when rock was something you did in a chair.

Old-timers will remember when a family that couldn't afford to own a car didn't.

An old-timer is someone who remembers when buying on time meant getting to the store before it closed.

An old-timer is someone who remembers when a woman looked the same after washing her face.

An old-timer is someone who can remember every detail of his life story, but can't remember how many times he's told it to the same person.

An old-timer is someone who remembers when a babysitter was called "mother."

An old-timer is someone who can remember when the height of indiscretion was to type a love letter.

✣

An old-timer is someone who can remember when money stayed around long enough for germs to grow on it.

✣

An old-timer is someone who remembers when we counted our blessings instead of our calories.

✣

An old-timer is someone who remembers when a child had more brothers and sisters than he had fathers.

✣

You're an old-timer if you can remember when the most popular family on the block was the one with the TV set.

✣

An old-timer is someone who could read a novel without having to hide it from the children each time he put it down.

✣

An old-timer is someone who can remember when getting his house debugged meant calling the insect exterminator.

✦

You're an old-timer if you remember when the only babes politicians kissed were those in their mothers' arms.

✦

An old-timer is someone who never had to look for his daughter when one of his shirts was missing.

✦

An old-timer is someone who can remember when a naughty child was taken to the woodshed instead of to a psychiatrist.

—*David Greenberg*

✦

An old-timer is someone who can remember when the wealthiest man in town owned a two-car garage.

✦

An old-timer is someone who remembers when you wouldn't upset anybody just by telling the truth.

20

Name-the-Year Quiz
No. 7

Name the Year
192__

In the News
- Fascism in Germany
- U.S. refuses to trade with Russia

New Products, Fads, and Fashion
- Eskimo Pies
- Westinghouse Home Radio
- Piggly Wiggly Stores
- Miss America contest
- First state tax—Virginia
- Tunic Bathing Suits

Music, Sports, and Entertainment
- Songs—"April Showers," "I'm Just Wild About Harry," "The Sheik of Araby"
- Jack Dempsey defeat
- Vincent Lopez—from the Hotel Pennsylvania Grill—radio

Name the Year
193__

In the News
- Little League baseball
- Blue Shield surgical plans
- First helicopter
- World War II begins

New Products, Fads, and Fashion
- Self-winding watches
- Paperback books
- Telephone booth packing
- The "Jitterbug" and the "Lindy" dances
- Babushkas
- Pillbox hats
- Pompadour hairdo

Music, Sports, and Entertainment
- Songs—"Moonlight Serenade," "Over the Rainbow," "In the Mood"
- New York Yankees win World Series in four straight games
- Bobby Riggs wins at Wimbledon
- The Glenn Miller Band becomes popular
- Frank Sinatra begins to become known
- "The Aldrich Family"—radio

Name the Year
194__

In the News
- Gasoline rationing

- Savings Bonds and Stamps
- Manhattan Atomic Research Project
- Pearl Harbor attacked

New Products, Fads, and Fashion
- Aerosol spray
- Women's broad-shouldered and mannish suits

Music, Sports, and Entertainment
- Songs—"Bewitched, Bothered, and Bewildered," "Blues in the Night," "Chattanooga Choo-Choo"
- Joe Louis knocks out Red Burman
- Eddie Arcaro rides Whirlaway to a Triple Crown
- Joe DiMaggio hits in 56 consecutive games
- Rita Hayworth becomes the "Love Goddess"
- "Mr. District Attorney," "Red Skelton Hour," "Arthur Godfrey Time"—radio

Name the Year
195__

In the News
- European Common Market
- Parents without Partners
- Videotape
- Soviets launch Sputnik I and II
- Great Britain explodes thermonuclear bomb in Pacific
- Billy Graham draws record crowds in Madison Square Garden

New Products, Fads, and Fashion
- Portable electric typewriter
- The Edsel automobile
- Frisbee throwing
- Flour sack look in dresses with a flat bow on the buttocks

Music, Sports, and Entertainment
- Songs—"Tammy," "Jailhouse Rock," "That'll Be the Day," "Kisses Sweeter Than Wine"
- America dances to calypso beat
- Buddy Holly and the Crickets
- Dick Clark becomes popular
- "American Bandstand," "Maverick," "Have Gun, Will Travel," "Perry Mason"—TV

Name the Year
196__

In the News
- Jogging Association
- Great Britain legalizes abortion
- Hong Kong flu
- Intelligence ship "Pueblo" seized by North Korea
- Draft resistance gains support
- Apollo 8 orbits the moon
- Jacqueline Kennedy marries Aristotle Onassis

New Products, Fads, and Fashion
- Fruit-flavored yogurts
- Nehru jackets and turtlenecks replace shirt and tie
- Pantsuits for women

Music, Sports, and Entertainment
- Songs—"Hey, Jude," "Mrs. Robinson," Scarborough Fair," "Eleanor Rigby," "California Dreamin'," "Hold Me Tight"
- U.S. takes 45 gold medals in Mexico City Summer Olympics
- Claude Killy takes gold medals in downhill skiing
- Rock 'n' roll here to stay
- Explicit sex common in films
- Beginning of film ratings
- "Laugh-In," "The Beautiful Phyllis Diller Show"—TV

21

Grins

Life would be infinitely happier if we could only be born at the age of 80 and gradually approach 18.

—*Mark Twain*

✢

I'm having a glorious old age. One of my greatest delights is that I have outlived most of my opposition.

—*Maggie Kuhn*

✢

Some of the happiest years of a woman's life are when she's 29.

✢

The best time for a man's ship to come in is before he's too old to navigate.

✢

Few woman admit their age. Few men act theirs.

✛

Children ask better questions than do adults.
"May I have a cookie?" "Why is the sky blue?"
and "What does a cow say?" are far more likely
to elicit a cheerful response than "Where's your
manuscript?" "Why haven't you called?" and
"Who's your lawyer?"

✛

Nothing ages a man faster than trying to prove
he's still as young as ever.

✛

Life is what happens to you while you are
making other plans.

—John Lennon

✛

Most elderly women were born in the year of
our Lord only knows.

✛

If you think a woman can't keep a secret, ask a
woman her age!

✛

Courage is what it takes for a woman to show
friends the old family Bible containing the date
of her birth.

✛

She recently had bad luck—she ran into someone she knew when they were the same age.

✛

Experience teaches you to recognize a mistake when you've made it again.

✛

We were planning to count the candles on his birthday cake . . . but we were driven back by the heat.

—*Stuart Turner*

✛

There's one advantage to being 102: There's no peer pressure.

—*Dennis Wolfberg*

✛

You can judge your age by the amount of pain you feel when you come in contact with a new idea.

✛

I don't age well. I never seem to get any older.

✢

"Don't worry about senility," my grandfather
used to say. "When it hits you, you won't know
it."

—*Bill Cosby*

✢

People who knew him 40 years ago say he still
looks like he looked then—old!

✢

Crossing the street in New York keeps old
people young—if they make it.

—*Andy Rooney*

✢

Jewelry takes people's minds off your wrinkles.

—*Sonja Henie*

✢

Some people will never live to be as old as they
look.

✢

You say you're 40? That's amazing! You still
look as though you're only 50.

✢

How can I die? I'm booked.

—*George Burns*

✛

About the only thing a woman is sure to remember is another woman's age.

✛

It's not true that women change their minds frequently. Ask a woman her age and she'll give you the same answer for several years.

✛

She's got so much bridgework that every time I kiss her I have to pay a toll.

✛

I have long thought that the aging process could be slowed down if it had to work its way through Congress.

—*George Bush*

✛

Forty is the most difficult age for a woman to pass. Sometimes it takes her ten years or more!

✛

Her age is her own business—and it looks like she's been in business a long time.

✛

The years that a woman subtracts from her age
are not lost. They are added to the ages of other
women.

—*Diane de Poitiers*

✛

If you want to learn a woman's real age, ask
someone who doesn't like her.

✛

My parents are having an age problem. He
won't act his and she won't tell hers.

✛

Some folks as they grow older grow wise, but
most folks simply grow stubborner.

—*Josh Billings*

✛

I advise you to go on living solely to enrage
those who are paying your annuities. It is the
only pleasure I have left.

✛

Years ago I thought old age would be dreadful,
because I should not be able to do things I

would want to do. Now I find there is nothing
I want to do after all.

—*Nancy Astor*

✛

Thirty-five is a very attractive age. London
society is full of women of the very highest birth
who have, of their own free choice, remained
35 for years.

—*Oscar Wilde*

✛

Her age is a millinery secret: She keeps it under
her hat.

✛

One should never trust a woman who tells one
her real age. A woman who would tell one that
would tell one anything.

—*Oscar Wilde*

✛

A man's as old as he's feeling, a woman as old
as she looks.

—*Mortimer Collins*

✛

When you are about 35 years old, something
terrible always happens to music.

—*Steve Race*

✦

My mother is going to have to stop lying about her age because pretty soon I'm going to be older than she is.

—*Tripp Evans*

✦

It is sobering to consider that when Mozart was my age (35), he had already been dead for a year.

—*Tom Lehrer*

✦

My wife says she's just turned 30—it was a U-turn.

✦

I've known her for many years—in fact, since we were the same age.

✦

Youthful figure: Something you get when you ask a woman her age.

✦

When I went to my class reunion, all the guys were so fat and bald they hardly recognized me.

✛

The average American woman is not old at 40—
in fact she isn't even 40.

✛

As you grow older you make a fool of yourself
in a more dignified manner.

✛

It's surprising how many persons our age are a
lot older than we are.

✛

She admitted she was 40 but she didn't say
when.

✛

I must be getting absentminded. Whenever I
complain that things aren't what they used to
be, I always forget to include myself.

—*George Burns*

✛

They tell you that you'll lose your mind when
you grow older. What they don't tell you is that
you won't miss it very much.

—*Malcolm Cowley*

✛

When I was very young I was disgracefully intolerant, but when I passed the 30 mark I prided myself on having learned the beautiful lesson that all things were good, and equally good. That, however, was really laziness. Now, thank goodness, I've sorted out what matters and what doesn't. And I'm beginning to be intolerant again.

—*G.B. Stern*

✛

I never lie about my age. I just tell people I'm as old as my wife—and then I lie about her age!

✛

"Girls" is what women over 45 call each other.

✛

They tell us that life begins at 40, but they don't say what kind of life.

✛

I was always told to respect my elders. It's just getting harder and harder to find one.

✛

The trouble with the Golden Rule is that before people are ready to live by it they have lead in their legs and silver in their hair.

✛

Twenty-five is always a nice age for a woman, especially if she happens to be 40.

✛

Which of you is going to step up and put me out to pasture?

—*John Wayne*

✛

I'm at an age when my back goes out more than I do.

—*Phyllis Diller*

✛

Life's golden age is when the children are too old to need babysitters and too young to borrow the family car.

✛

In youth, everything seems possible; but we reach a point in the middle years when we realize that we are never going to reach all the shining goals we had set for ourselves. And in

the end, most of us reconcile ourselves, with what grace we can, to living with our ulcers and arthritis, our sense of partial failure, our less-than-ideal families—and even our politicians!
—*Adlai E. Stevenson*

✛

Her birthday cake had so many candles on it she was fined for air pollution.

✛

You can tell she's 40. Just count the rings under her eyes.

✛

A man is usually as young as he feels but seldom as important.

✛

I have always felt that a woman has the right to treat the subject of her age with ambiguity until, perhaps, she passes into the realm of over 90. Then it is better she be candid with herself and with the world.
—*Helena Rubinstein*

✛

Nobody is harder on a woman's age than another woman guessing it.

22

Fountain of Youth

Youth is a wonderful thing; what a crime to
waste it on children.

> —*George Bernard Shaw*

✣

There is nothing wrong with the younger generation that the older generation didn't outgrow.

✣

We are only young once. That is all society can
stand.

✣

Many young men don't believe in standing on
their own two feet as long as they can ride on
four wheels.

✣

Children are a great comfort in your old age,
and they help you reach it faster, too.

> —*Lionel Kaufman*

✛

Remember now thy Creator in the days of thy youth, while the evil days come not, nor the years draw nigh, when thou shalt say, "I have no pleasure in them."

—*Ecclesiastes 12:1*

✛

There's not much wrong with the younger generation that becoming a parent and a taxpayer won't cure.

✛

Today's youth has very special problems—like the girl who lost one of her contact lenses in her boyfriend's beard.

✛

The accent may be on youth these days, but the stress is still on the parents.

✛

To keep young, stay around young people. To get old, try to keep up with them.

✛

The younger generation knows more about everything than the old folks—except making a living.

✦

The young have no depth perception in time. Ten years back or ten years forward is an eternity.

—*Robert C. Alberts*

✦

The average child is an almost nonexistent myth. To be normal one must be peculiar in some way or another.

—*Heywood Broun*

✦

Adolescence is just one big walking pimple.

—*Carol Burnett*

✦

Youth is a continual intoxication; it is the fever of reason.

—*François de la Rochefoucauld*

✦

If youth be a defect, it is one that we outgrow only too soon.

—*James Russell Lowell*

✦

Almost everything that is great has been done by youth.

—*Benjamin Disraeli*

✛

No young man believes he shall ever die.

—*William Hazlitt*

✛

The feeling that will never come back any-more—the feeling that I could last forever, out-last the sea, the earth, and all men.

—*Joseph Conrad*

✛

The typical American youth is always ready to give those who are older than himself the full benefit of his inexperience.

✛

Children need love, especially when they do not deserve it.

—*Harold S. Hulbert*

✛

Youths have a tremendous advantage over their elders in possessing the power of vision without the drawback of retrospect.

—*Henry Ford*

✛

In this life the old believe everything, the middle-aged suspect everything, and the young know everything.

✛

It's all that the young can do for the old to shock them and keep them up-to-date.
—*George Bernard Shaw*

✛

Life as yet untouched by tragedy.
—*Alfred North Whitehead*

✛

[They who] embrace more than they can hold, stir more than they can quiet, fly to the end without consideration of the means.
—*Francis Bacon*

✛

Young people are often bad because their parents did not burn their britches behind them.

✛

I am not young enough to know everything.
—*James M. Baffie*

✢

If you want to recapture your youth, just cut off
his allowance.

—*Al Bernstein*

✢

Let no man despise thy youth.

—*1 Timothy 4:12*

✢

This is a youth-oriented society, and the joke is
on them because youth is a disease from which
we all recover.

✢

It is better to be a young june bug than an old
bird-of-paradise.

—*Mark Twain*

✢

It is not possible for civilization to flow back-
wards while there is youth in the world.

—*Helen Keller*

✢

Older men declare war. But it is the youth that
must fight and die.

—*Herbert Hoover*

✢

When I was a child, I spoke as a child, I understood as a child, I thought as a child; but when I became a man, I put away childish things.
— *1 Corinthians 13:11* NKJV

✢

Youth today must be strong, unafraid, and a better taxpayer than its father.

✢

Youth comes but once in a lifetime.
— *Henry Wadsworth Longfellow*

✢

Of all virtues, the virtue of patience is most foreign to youth.

— *John Jay Chapman*

✢

In general my children refused to eat anything that hadn't danced on TV.

— *Erma Bombeck*

✢

Youth is a gift of nature, but age is a work of art.
— *Garson Kanin*

✢

Being young is a fault which improves daily.

✢

The young think they know everything and are confident in their assertions.

—Aristotle

✢

Young men have a passion for regarding their elders as senile.

—Henry Adams

✢

Beautiful is youth because it never comes again.
—George Jean Nathan

✢

What you long for in youth you get aplenty in old age.

—Goethe

✢

Being young is beautiful, but being old is comfortable.

—Ebner-Eschenbach

✠

To get back one's youth, one has merely to repeat one's follies.

—*Oscar Wilde*

✠

In youth we clothe ourselves with rainbows.

—*Emerson*

✠

What is more enchanting than the voices of young people when you can't hear what they say?

—*Logan Pearsall Smith*

✠

Youth is a disease that must be borne with patiently! Time, indeed, will cure it.

—*R.H. Benson*

✠

The youth of a nation are the trustees of posterity.

—*Benjamin Disraeli*

✠

The young always have the same problem—how to rebel and conform at the same time. They have now solved this by defying their parents and copying one another.

—*Quentin Crisp*

✦

The denunciation of the young is a necessary
part of the hygiene of older people, and greatly
assists the circulation of the blood.
—*Logan Pearsall Smith*

✦

There is nothing that can pay one for that
invaluable ignorance which is the companion
of youth; those sanguine groundless hopes, and
that lively vanity, which make all the happiness
of life.
—*Lady Mary Wortley Montagu*

✦

It is absurd to talk of the ignorance of youth.
The only people to whose opinions I listen now
with any respect are people much younger than
myself. They seem in front of me.
—*Oscar Wilde*

✦

If youth is a fault, one soon gets rid of it.
—*Goethe*

✦

Youth is the period in which a man can be hope-
less. The end of every episode is the end of the
world. But the power of hoping through every-

thing, the knowledge that the soul survives its adventures, that great inspiration comes to the middle-aged.

—G.K. Chesterton

✢

Youth is a period of missed opportunities.

—Cyril Connolly

✢

Towering in the confidence of 21.

—Dr. Samuel Johnson

✢

Don't laugh at a youth for his affectations; he's only trying on one face after another till he finds his own.

—Logan Pearsall Smith

✢

What the vast majority of American children need is to stop being pampered, stop being indulged, stop being chauffeured, stop being catered to. In the final analysis it is not what you do for your children but what you have taught them to do for themselves that will make them successful human beings.

—Ann Landers

23

Name-the-Year Quiz
No. 8

Name the Year
192__

In the News
- Charles Lindbergh's solo flight to Paris
- Academy of Motion Picture Arts
- "The Jazz Singer"—first talking movie

New Products, Fads, and Fashion
- Handset telephones
- Iron lung
- Hydraulic shock absorbers for cars
- The words "racket" and "racketeering" enter the American vocabulary
- Straight clothes with no curves

Music, Sports, and Entertainment
- Songs—"My Blue Heaven," "Let a Smile Be Your Umbrella," "Ol' Man River"
- Babe Ruth's greatest home run year
- "Two Black Crows"—radio

Name the Year
193__

In the News
- Unemployment insurance
- Charles and Ann Lindbergh's baby is kidnapped
- John Dillinger becomes famous
- Gandhi is arrested again

New Products, Fads, and Fashion
- Ford V-8
- Marathon dancing (24 weeks and five days—longest dance)
- Popeye's expression "I yam what I yam" becomes popular

Music, Sports, and Entertainment
- Songs—"I'm Getting Sentimental over You," "Night and Day," "April in Paris"
- Lou Gehrig hits four home runs
- Duke Ellington a serious jazz composer
- Fred Allen, Jack Benny, Mary Livingstone, Burns and Allen—radio
- "One Man's Family," "Vic and Sade," "Just Plain Bill," "Pepper Young's Family"

Name the Year
194__

In the News
- The atom bomb—Hiroshima and Nagasaki
- Glass-dome railroad cars

- Fluoride in drinking water
- Roosevelt, Churchill, and Stalin meet at Yalta
- Hitler believed to commit suicide
- U.S. bomber crashes into Empire State Building

New Products, Fads, and Fashion
- *Seventeen* magazine for teens
- Fashions for teenage girls

Music, Sports, and Entertainment
- Songs—"Laura," "June Is Bustin' Out All Over," "These Foolish Things"
- Vladimir Horowitz plays "The Stars and Stripes Forever"
- Ernie Pyle becomes popular war correspondent
- "Meet The Press," "The Danny Kaye Show," "Beulah," "Queen for a Day"—radio

Name the Year
195__

In the News
- U.S. reactor testing station
- Estes Kefauver investigates organized crime
- Julius and Ethel Rosenberg sentenced to die by electrocution for selling atom-bomb secrets to Russia
- President Truman fires Gen. Douglas MacArthur

New Products, Fads, and Fashion
- Bank credit cards
- Long-distance dialing
- Power steering for cars
- Commercial color television
- Poodle haircut
- Capezio shoes become popular

Music, Sports, and Entertainment
- Songs—"Getting to Know You," "Come on-a My House," "On Top of Old Smoky"
- Joe DiMaggio retires from baseball
- Jersey Joe Walcott wins heavyweight title from Ezzard Charles
- "Search for Tomorrow," "Love of Life," "See It Now," "People Are Funny," "Kraft Theatre," "Studio One"—TV

Name the Year
196__

In the News
- Amnesty International
- Dr. Timothy Leary wants to legalize drugs
- Medicare
- Cultural revolution in China—The Red Guard
- "Black Power"

New Products, Fads, and Fashion
- The word "psychedelic"
- 8-track stereo cassette recorders in Ford cars

Music, Sports, and Entertainment
- Billie Jean King wins at Wimbledon
- Cassius Clay still the champ
- John Lennon claims that the Beatles are more popular than Jesus
- The Mamas and the Papas and Neil Diamond become popular
- "The Dating Game," "Star Trek," "Dark Shadows"—TV

24

Oldies but Goodies

Age is the best possible fire extinguisher for flaming youth.

✢

Aging is at work when your kids study in history what you used to study as current events.

✢

Age is like love; it cannot be hidden.

✢

Old age has its pleasures, which, though different, are not less than the pleasures of youth.
—*W. Somerset Maugham*

✢

Old age is like climbing a mountain. You climb from ledge to ledge. The higher you get, the more tired and breathless you become, but your view becomes much more extensive.

—*Ingmar Bergman*

✛

Age: By the time a man is wise enough to watch his step, he's too old to go anywhere.

✛

It's wonderful to grow old, if you can remember to stay young while you're doing it.

✛

Yes, autumn is really the best of the seasons; and I'm not sure that old age isn't the best part of life. But of course, like autumn, it doesn't last.

✛

We old folks know more about being young than young folks know about being old.

✛

That time of life when we convince ourselves it's only a vitamin deficiency.

✛

Age does not depend upon years, but upon temperament and health. Some people are born old, and some never grow so.

✢

As for wrinkles—pshaw! Why shouldn't we have wrinkles? Honorable insignia of long service in this warfare.

✢

In youth the days are short and the years are long; in old age the years are short and the days long.

—*Panin*

✢

Old age doesn't keep men from chasing women; they just have trouble remembering why.

✢

Take care that old age does not wrinkle your spirit even more than your face.

—*Michel de Montaigne*

✢

I'm not interested in age. People who tell their age are silly. You're as young as you feel.

—*Elizabeth Arden*

✦

Growing old is like being increasingly penalized for a crime you haven't committed.

—*Anthony Powell*

✦

You can't win. When you get too old for pimples, you go right into wrinkles.

✦

To make success of old age a fellow sure has to start young.

✦

The older we get, the fewer things seem worth waiting in line for.

✦

One of the privileges of old age is to relate experiences that nobody will believe and give advice that nobody will follow.

✦

Old age is when you get enough exercise just trying to stay out of the way.

✛

The best thing about old age is that a person only has to go through it once.

✛

Don't resent growing old—many are denied the privilege.

✛

Old age is the time of life when wisdom and stubbornness are often mistaken for each other.

✛

He's so old he gets winded playing chess.

✛

If you can't grow old gracefully, do it any way you can.

✛

To grow older is a new venture in itself.
—*Goethe*

✛

Old age is something everybody else reaches before you do.

✤

Old age is when your idea of getting ahead is just to stay even.

✤

Old age has overtaken a man when he has to run to go as fast as he used to walk.

✤

Why do folks make such a fuss about growing old? All it takes is a little time!

✤

The trouble with growing old is that there's not much future in it.

✤

It's funny how we never get too old to learn some new ways to be foolish.

✤

By the time old people decide it's wise to watch their step, they aren't going anywhere.

✤

Most old people enjoy living in the past. It's cheaper.

✛

The reason old folks enjoy living in the past is because it's larger than their future.

✛

One of the nice things about growing old is that, with all the emphasis on youth, you can go pretty much unnoticed.

✛

About the only thing that comes to him who waits is old age.

✛

My old sister tells me she has discovered a wonderful way to eliminate wrinkles: "When you look in the mirror take off your glasses."

✛

One nice thing about being old: As the noise level goes up, your hearing goes down.

✛

You're aging when you start to look for your name in the obituary column.

✛

Age stiffens the joints and thickens some brains.

✛

I begin to realize that I am growing old: The taxi driver calls me "Pop" instead of "Buddy."

—*Alexander Woollcott*

✛

Growing old—it's not nice, but it's interesting.

—*August Strindberg*

✛

"Age" is the acceptance of a term of years. But maturity is the glory of years.

—*Martha Graham*

✛

Age is so deceiving. It is amazing how much faster 60 comes after 50 compared to 50 after 40!

✛

The greatest compensation of old age is its freedom of spirit. . . . Another compensation is that it liberates you from envy, hatred, and malice.

—*W. Somerset Maugham*

25

Time to Retire

The problem with being retired is that you never know what day it is, what time it is, where you're supposed to be, or what you're supposed to be doing. It's a lot like working for the government.

✝

Cessation of work is not accompanied by cessation of expenses.

—*Cato*

✝

Don't think of retiring from the world until the world will be sorry that you retire. I hate a fellow whom pride or cowardice or laziness drives into a corner, and who does nothing when he is there but sit and growl. Let him come out as I do, and bark

—*Samuel Johnson*

✝

Nothing is more usual than the sight of old people who yearn for retirement, and nothing is so rare as those who have retired and do not regret it.

—*Charles De Saint-Evremond*

✢

I really think it's better to retire when you still have some snap left in your garters.

—*Russell B. Long*

✢

Retired is being tired twice, I've thought—first tired of working, then tired of not.

—*Richard Armour*

✢

The fellow who can't figure out what to do with a Sunday afternoon is often the same one who can't wait for retirement.

✢

When some fellers decide to retire, nobody knows the difference.

—*Kin Hubbard*

✢

The best time to start thinking about your retirement is before the boss does.

✛

A man is known by the company that keeps him on after retirement age.

✛

Retirement is the ugliest word in the language.
—*Ernest Hemingway*

✛

He still has some difficulty adjusting to retirement. Every morning he struggles downstairs to the kitchen and punches his time card in the toaster.

✛

Since his retirement, he's started a career in the take-out business. His wife tells him every day, "Take out the garbage . . . take out the dog . . . take out the weeds."

✛

A male retiree says he's been playing golf occasionally—but only on days ending with *y*.

✛

We have reached the point where too many folks want to retire before they go to work.

✢

Retirement is wonderful if you have two essentials—much to live on and much to live for.

✢

You know you're ready for retirement when you take off your shoes, put on your slippers, and even they hurt.

✢

Retirement is when you sit around and watch the sunset—if you can stay up that late.

✢

Retirement is when a man who figured he'd go fishing seven times a week finds himself washing the dishes three times a day.

✢

Retirement takes all the fun out of Saturdays.
—*Duke Gmahle*

✢

Always plan your future in such a way that when the time comes to put out to pasture you will be able to choose your own grazing grounds.

✛

Retirement is when the living is easy and the payments are hard.

✛

Two weeks is about the ideal length of time to retire.

—Alex Comfort

✛

Why is it that when you retire and time is no longer so important, they give you a watch?

✛

Retirement means twice as much husband on half as much money.

✛

He's at that difficult stage in life where he's too old to work and too poor to retire.

✛

The first big shock of retirement is when you realize that there are no days off.

✛

Retirement won't change you that much. You'll find that all those things that you never had time to do become all those things that you don't have the money to do.

✛

Sixty-five is the age when one acquires sufficient experience to lose his job.

✛

There are a lot of books telling you how to manage when you retire. What most people want is one that'll tell them how to manage in the meantime.

✛

Experience is what you've got when you're too old to get a job.

✛

One of the problems of retirement is that it gives you more time to read about the problems of retirement.

✛

Don't simply retire from something; have something to retire to.

—*Harry Emerson Fosdick*

✛

Retirement is when your wife realizes she never gave your secretary enough sympathy.

✛

Retirement security is making sure all the doors are locked before you go to bed.

✛

Before deciding to retire from your job, stay home a week and watch daytime television.

✛

Retirement is the time of life when you stop lying about your age and start lying about the house.

✛

The worst thing about retirement is having to drink coffee on your own time.

✛

A recent retiree writes that he's tired of retirement already: "I wake up in the morning with nothing to do, and by bedtime I have it only half done."

✛

Many a retired husband becomes his wife's full-time job.

✛

Forty years ago when a fellow said something about retiring, he was talking about going to bed.

✛

Most people perform essentially meaningless work. When they retire, that truth is borne in upon them.

—*Brendan Francis*

✛

Few men of action have been able to make a graceful exit at the appropriate time.

—*Malcolm Muggeridge*

✛

Have you ever been out for a late autumn walk in the closing part of the afternoon, and suddenly looked up to realize that the leaves have practically all gone? And the sun has set and the day gone before you knew it—and with that a cold wind blows across the landscape? That's retirement.

—*Stephen Leacock*

✛

I'll take any job that gets me out of the house.
My husband retired yesterday.

✛

I get a regular monthly pension. The money
may not be much, but the working conditions
are terrific!

✛

An ancient myth teaches that at creation the
dog, the horse, the monkey, and human beings
were given 40 years each to live on this earth.
The dog, the horse, and the monkey said, "We
don't need all that time to live." So they each
gave man ten years of their allotted 40 years.

Now you know why man leads a dog's life
between 40 and 50, works like a horse between
50 and 60, and after that just monkeys around.

26

Name-the-Year Quiz
No. 9

Name the Year
192__

In the News
- Mussolini marches on Rome
- King Tutankhamen's tomb discovered
- Insulin discovered

New Products, Fads, and Fashion
- *Reader's Digest*
- Balloon tires
- 60,000 radios owned
- Women began to smoke in public
- Emily Post's book on etiquette

Music, Sports, and Entertainment
- Songs—"My Buddy," "Toot, Toot, Tootsie," "Chicago"
- Babe Ruth becomes outfielder for Yankees
- Charles Atlas is "World's Most Perfectly Developed Man"
- George Burns and Gracie Allen
- Rudy Vallee becomes popular
- Paul Whiteman, "King of Jazz"—radio
- Lucky Strike Radio Show

Name the Year
193__

In the News
- U.S. Social Security System
- Alcoholics Anonymous
- Luftwaffe is formed
- Italy invades Ethiopia
- Persia becomes Iran
- Works Progress Administration (WPA)
- Will Rogers and Wiley Post killed in Alaska in a plane crash

New Products, Fads, and Fashion
- 35-mm Kodachrome film
- Parking meters
- Little Audrey stories
- The rumba becomes fashionable
- Monopoly is a hit
- Hair short and softly waved
- Hat tipped over right eye

Music, Sports, and Entertainment
- Songs—"Begin the Beguine," "I Got Plenty of Nothing," "Just One of Those Things"
- Jesse Owens breaks three world track records
- Babe Ruth retires from active play
- Bandleader Ozzie Nelson marries singer Harriet Hilliard
- "Your Hit Parade," "Cavalcade of America," "Lights Out," "Fibber McGee and Molly," "One Man's Family," "Major Bowes Amateur Hour," Jack Benny—radio

Name the Year
194__

In the News
- U.S. Women's Army Corps(WACS), Women's Naval WAVES, Women's Coast Guard SPARS
- The Armed Forces Radio Service
- Penicillin
- The bazooka
- Lt. Col. James Doolittle raids Tokyo with B-25 bombers
- Douglas MacArthur Supreme Commander of Southwest Pacific area
- Gen. Erwin Rommel, "the Desert Fox"
- Japanese-Americans in internment camps
- Food rationing

New Products, Fads, and Fashion
- First true computer
- Silicone
- Men's trousers are cuffless
- Leather shoes are replaced by canvas shoes

Music, Sports, and Entertainment
- Songs—"Deep in the Heart of Texas," "That Old Black Magic," "Don't Sit Under an Apple Tree"
- Joe Louis knocks out Buddy Baer in one round
- Woody Herman, Kay Kyser, Charlie Spivak, Sammy Kaye, Count Basie, and Artie Shaw become very popular

• Edward R. Murrow, Eric Sevareid, William L. Shirer, Bill Henry, and Elmer Davis—radio

Name the Year
195__

In the News
• Rocket-powered plane flies 1600 mph
• Dwight D. Eisenhower becomes president
• Joseph Stalin dies
• Sir Edmund P. Hillary climbs Mount Everest with Sherpa guide Tenzing Norgay

New Products, Fads, and Fashion
• Liquid rouge
• 3-D fad
• Scrabble catches on
• Dacron wash-and-wear
• Bermuda shorts with knee socks
• Short Italian haircuts
• Blanket ponchos

Music, Sports, and Entertainment
• Songs—"Vaya Con Dios," "Your Cheatin' Heart," "How Much Is That Doggie in the Window?"
• New York Yankees take World Series from Brooklyn Dodgers
• Arthur Godfrey fires Julius LaRosa
• "I Love Lucy," "Goodyear Playhouse," "Person to Person," "The Adventures of Superman," "The Life of Riley," "Danny Kaye Show"—TV

Name the Year
196__

In the News
- Hot line between Washington and Moscow
- Dr. Michael De Bakey and the artificial heart
- John F. Kennedy assassinated in Dallas
- Jack Ruby murders Lee Harvey Oswald
- Dr. Timothy Leary discharged for experiments with LSD
- Martin Luther King Jr.'s "I Have a Dream" speech

New Products, Fads, and Fashion
- Cassette recorder
- Color Polaroid cameras
- "Tom Swift" jokes

Music, Sports, and Entertainment
- Songs—"Blowin' in the Wind," "Puff, the Magic Dragon," "Call Me Irresponsible," "If I Had a Hammer"
- Jack Nicklaus wins the Masters
- Surfing begins to spawn a subculture
- Bob Dylan, Joan Baez, Barbara Streisand, and Stevie Wonder become popular
- "The Fugitive," "Chrysler Theater" with Bob Hope—TV

27

Sage Advice

The immature man wants to die nobly for a cause, while the mature man wants to live humanely for one.

—*Wilheim Stekel*

✛

More people would live to a ripe old age if they weren't too busy providing for it.

✛

There is nothing more remarkable in the life of Socrates than that he found time in his old age to learn to dance and play on instruments, and thought it was time well spent.

—*Michel de Montaigne*

✛

Anyone who stops learning is old, whether at 20 or 80. Anyone who keeps learning stays young. The greatest thing in life is to keep your mind young.

—*Henry Ford*

✝

I enjoy my wrinkles and regard them as badges
of distinction—I've worked hard for them!

—*Maggie Kuhn*

✝

A man is not old until regrets take the place of
dreams.

—*John Barrymore*

✝

As we advance in life, we acquire a keener sense
of the value of time. Nothing else, indeed,
seems of any consequence; and we become
misers in this respect.

—*William Hazlitt*

✝

Age does not protect you from love. But love, to
some extent, protects you from age.

✝

If wrinkles must be written upon our brows, let
them not be written upon the heart. The spirit
should never grow old.

—*James A. Garfield*

✛

A man is not old as long as he is seeking something.

—*Jean Rostand*

✛

With the ancient is wisdom, and in length of days understanding.

—*Job 12:12*

✛

To keep the heart unwrinkled, to be hopeful, kindly, cheerful, reverent—that is to triumph over old age.

—*Thomas Bailey Aldrich*

✛

Grow up, and that is a terribly hard thing to do. It is much easier to skip it and go from one childhood to another.

—*F. Scott Fitzgerald*

✛

The greatest problem about old age is the fear that it may go on too long.

—*A. J. P. Taylor*

✛

He who devotes 16 hours a day to hard study
may become as wise at 60 as he thought himself
at 20.
—Mary Wilson Little

✛

When we grow old, there can only be one
regret: not to have given enough of ourselves.
—Eleonora Duse

✛

Old age is the most unexpected of all things that
happen to a man.
—Leon Trotsky

✛

There is nothing more beautiful in this world
than a healthy, wise old man.
—Lin Yutang

✛

Forty is the old age of youth; 50 is the youth of
old age.
—Victor Hugo

✛

Age imprints more wrinkles in the mind than it
does on the face.
—Montaigne

✜

Old age has a great sense of calm and freedom. When the passions have relaxed their hold you have escaped, not from one master, but from many.

—*Plato*

✜

The illusion that [the] times that were are better than those that are has probably pervaded all ages.

—*Horace Greeley*

✜

The older I get, the more wisdom I find in the ancient rule of taking first things first—a process which often reduces the most complex human problems to manageable proportions.
—*Dwight D. Eisenhower*

✜

Old and new make the warp and woof of every moment. There is no thread that is not a twist of these two strands.

—*Ralph Waldo Emerson*

✜

I am long on ideas, but short on time. I expect to live to be only about a hundred.
—*Thomas A. Edison*

✢

We don't grow older, we grow riper.
                    —*Pablo Picasso*

✢

Many foxes grow gray, but few grow good.
                    —*Benjamin Franklin*

✢

No one grows old by living—only by losing interest in living.

                    —*Marie Ray*

I promise to keep on living as though I expected to live forever. Nobody grows old by merely living a number of years. People grow old only by deserting their ideals. Years may wrinkle the skin, but to give up interest wrinkles the soul.
                    —*Gen. Douglas MacArthur*

✢

It gives me great pleasure to converse with the aged. They have been over the road that all of us must travel, and know where it is rough and difficult and where it is level and easy.

                    —*Plato*

✛

When I was young I pitied the old. Now old, it is the young I pity.

—*Jean Rostand*

✛

When I was a child, nobody died; but now it happens all the time.

✛

Some old women and men grow bitter with age. The more their teeth drop out the more biting they get.

—*George Dennison Prentice*

✛

It's not that age brings childhood back again. Age merely shows what children we remain.

—*Goethe*

✛

When grace is joined with wrinkles, it is adorable. There is an unspeakable dawn in happy old age.

—*Victor Hugo*

✛

If I had my life to live over again, I would start barefoot earlier in the spring.

✢

An old man in a house is a good sign.
                        —*Benjamin Franklin*

✢

To know how to grow old is the master work of
wisdom, and one of the most difficult chapters
in the great art of living.
                        —*Frederic Amiel*

✢

In growing old, we become more foolish—and
more wise.
                        —*François de la Rochefoucauld*

✢

Our youth we can have but today; we may
always find time to grow old.
                        —*George Berkeley*

✢

An old man loved is winter with flowers.

✢

Growing old is no more than a bad habit which
a busy man has not time to form.
                        —*Andre Maurois*

✛

Lord, Lord! How subject we old men are to this vice of lying.

—*William Shakespeare*

✛

The first 40 years of life give us the text; the next 30 supply the commentary.

—*Arthur Schopenhauer*

✛

When I grow up, I want to be a little boy.

—*Joseph Heller*

✛

Q: What's the difference between the young and the old?
A: The young don't know what to do, while the old can't do what they know.

✛

The man who views the world at 50 the same as he did at 20 has wasted 30 years of his life.

—*Mohammed Ali*

✛

We have not passed that subtle line between childhood and adulthood until we move from

the passive voice to the active voice—that is,
until we have stopped saying "It got lost" and
say "I lost it."

—*Sydney J. Harris*

✛

The greatest thing about getting older is that
you don't lose all the other ages you've been.
—*Madeleine L'Engle*

✛

Bliss was it in that dawn to be alive, but to be
young was very heaven!

—*William Wordsworth*

✛

No one is so old as to think he cannot live one
more year.

—*Cicero*

✛

In youth we run into difficulties; in old age difficulties run into us.

—*Josh Billings*

✛

Every man desires to live long, but no man
would be old.

—*Jonathan Swift*

✛

It is always self-defeating to pretend to the style of a generation younger than your own; it simply erases your own experience in history.
—*Renata Adler*

✛

During the first period of a man's life the greatest danger is not to take the risk.
—*S.A. Kierkegaard*

✛

The years in your life are less important than the life in your years.

✛

He wears the rose of youth upon him.
—*William Shakespeare*

✛

To know how to grow old is the master-work of wisdom, and one of the most difficult chapters in the great art of living.
—*Henri Frederic Amiel*

✛

When you were born, you cried and the world rejoiced. Live your life in such a manner that when you die, the world cries and you rejoice.

✛

The worst thing, I fear, about being no longer young is that one is no longer young.

—*Harold Nicolson*

✛

Before you contradict an old man, my fair friend, you should endeavor to understand him.

—*George Santayana*

✛

I really believe that more harm is done by old men who cling to their influence than by young men who anticipate it.

—*Owen D. Young*

✛

Perhaps our anger at the younger generation is misplaced; Diogenes struck the father when the son swore.

✛

There are so few who can grow old with a good grace.

—*Richard Steele*

A man over 90 is a great comfort to all his elderly neighbors: He is a picket-guard at the extreme outpost; and the young folks of 60 and 70 feel that the enemy must get by him before he can come near their camp.
—*Oliver Wendell Holmes Jr*

At 20 a man thinks he can save the world. At 40 he's lucky if he can save part of his salary.

I want to die young at a ripe old age.
—*Ashley Montagu*

28

Ageless Verse

As a white candle in a holy place,
So is the beauty of an aged face.
                                   —*Joseph Campbell*

✢

I adore my bifocals, my false teeth fit fine.
My hairpiece fits swell, but I sure miss my
mind.

✢

It's sad for a girl to reach the age where men
consider her charmless; but it's worse for a man
to attain the age when girls consider him harm-
less.

✢

Men are like wine, aged in wood;
Age sours the bad, betters the good.

✢

Forty years on,
Growing older and older,
Shorter in wind, as in memory long,

Feeble of foot, and rheumatic of shoulder,
What will it help you that once you were
strong?

—*E.E. Bowen*

✣

Senescence begins
And middle age ends
The day your descendants
Outnumber your friends.

✣

At ten, a child; at twenty, wild;
At thirty, tame, if ever;
At forty, wise; at fifty, rich;
At sixty, good, or never.

✣

Where is the heart that doth not keep
Within its inmost core
Some fond remembrance hidden deep
Of days that are no more?

—*Ellen Clementine Howarth*

✣

Seventy is wormwood,
Seventy is gall,
But it's better to be seventy
Than not alive at all.

—*Phyllis McGinley*

✛

I grow old ... I grow old ...
I shall wear the bottoms of my trousers rolled.
—*T.S. Eliot*

✛

Make your wife happy; it's easily done:
Remember her birthday but forget which one.

✛

Of late I appear
To have reached that stage
When people look old
Who are only my age.

—*Richard Armour*

✛

I have a bone to pick with Fate;
Come here and tell me, girlie,
Do you think my mind is maturing late,
Or simply rotted early?

—*Ogden Nash*

✛

I never forgot a face or a name;
The bothersome thing in my case is:
The names I remember are seldom the same
As those that belong with the faces.

✛

The face I see is furrowed now;
In fact, it's rather rutty.
Revlon and Clinique won't do—
I need a can of putty!

—*J.T.N.*

✛

I'm growing fonder of my staff;
I'm growing dimmer in the eyes;
I'm growing fainter in my laugh;
I'm growing deeper in my sighs;
I'm growing careless of my dress;
I'm growing frugal of my gold;
I'm growing wise;
I'm growing ... yes ...
I'm growing old.

—*J.G. Saxe*

✛

A little more tired at close of day,
A little less anxious to have our way;
A little less ready to scold and blame,
A little more care of a brother's name;
And so we are nearing our journey's end,
Where time and eternity meet and blend.

—*Rollin John Wells*

✤

When that old joke was new
   It was not hard to joke,
And puns we now pooh-pooh
   Great laughter would provoke.

True wit was seldom heard
   And humor shown by few,
When reigned King George the Third,
   And that old joke was new.

It passed indeed for wit,
   Did this achievement rare,
When down your friend would sit,
   To steal away his chair.

You brought him to the floor,
   You bruised him black and blue,
And this would cause a roar,
   When your old joke was new.
               —*W.M. Thackeray*

✤

I'm fine, I'm fine.
There's nothing whatever the matter with me.
I'm just as healthy as I can be.
I have arthritis in both of my knees.
And when I talk, I talk with a wheeze.
My pulse is weak and my blood is thin,
But I'm awfully well for the shape I'm in.
My teeth eventually will have to come out,
And I can't hear a word unless you shout.
I'm overweight and I can't get thin,

But I'm awfully well for the shape I'm in.
Arch supports I have for both feet
Or I wouldn't be able to walk down the street.
Sleep is denied me every night,
And every morning I'm really a sight.
My memory is bad and my head's a-spin,
And I practically live on aspirin,
But I'm awfully well for the shape I'm in.
The moral is, as this tale unfolds,
That for you and me who are growing old,
It's better to say "I'm fine" with a grin
Than to let people know the shape we're in!

+

It Got Up and Went

How do I know my youth is all spent?
My get-up and go has got up and went.
My joints are still and filled with pain.
The pills that I take, they give me no gain.
I rub in the ointment, like fury I do,
Each pain when it leaves comes back with two.

But in spite of it all I am able to grin
When I think of the places my get-up has been.
Old age is golden, I have heard said,
But sometimes I wonder as I get into bed—
My "ears" on the dresser, my "teeth" in a cup,
My "eyes" on the table until I wake up.
Ere sleep comes each night I say to myself,
"Is there anything else I should lay on the shelf?"
Yet I am happy to know as I close the door,
My friends are the same as in days of yore.

Since I have retired from life's competition
Each day is filled with complete repetition.
I get up every morning and dust off my wits,
Go pick up the paper and read the "o-bits."
If my name isn't there I know I'm not dead;
I get a good breakfast and go back to bed.
The reason I know my youth is all spent—
My get-up-and-go has got up and went.

✣

We climbed to the top of Goat Point hill,
    Sweet Kitty, my sweetheart, and I,
And watched the moon make stars on the waves,
    And the dim white ships go by,
While a throne we made on a rough stone wall,
    And the king and the queen were we;
And I sat with my arm about Kitty,
    And she with her arm about me.

The water was mad in the moonlight,
    And the sand like gold where it shone,
And our hearts kept time to its music
    As we sat in the splendor alone.
And Kitty's dear eyes twinkled brightly
    And Kitty's brown hair blew so free,
While I sat with my arm about Kitty,
    And she with her arm about me.

Last night we drove in our carriage
    To the wall at the top of the hill;
And though we're 40 years older,
    We're children and sweetheart still.
And we talked again of that moonlight
    That danced so mad on the sea,

When I sat with my arm about Kitty,
　　And she with her arm about me.

The throne on the wall was still standing,
　　But we sat in the carriage last night,
For a wall is too high for old people
　　Whose foreheads have linings of white.
And Kitty's waist measure is forty,
　　While mine is full fifty and three,
So I can't get my arm about Kitty,
　　Nor can she get both hers around me.
　　　　　　　　　　　—H.H. Porter

29

Name-the-Year Quiz
No. 10

Name the Year
192__

In the News
- Hitler reorganizes Nazi party
- Scopes trial on evolution

New Products, Fads, and Fashion
- *New Yorker* magazine
- Dry ice
- Ford cars in colors other than black
- Dance marathons
- The dance called "the shimmy"
- Flapper dresses
- Strap pumps

Music, Sports, and Entertainment
- Songs—"Show Me the Way to Go Home," "Five Foot Two, Eyes of Blue," "Yes, Sir, That's My Baby"
- Red Grange becomes captain of Illinois football team

- "Atwater Kent Program," "The Grand Ol' Opry"—radio

Name the Year
193__

In the News
- Shirley Temple
- John Dillinger is gunned down
- Baby Face Nelson becomes public enemy number one
- Bonnie and Clyde are shot to death

New Products, Fads, and Fashion
- Fluorescent lighting
- Little Big Books
- Soap Box Derby
- Skiing becomes popular
- Seersucker summer suits for men

Music, Sports, and Entertainment
- Songs—"Blue Moon," "On the Good Ship Lollipop," "Cocktails for Two"
- Max Baer becomes heavyweight champ
- Red Grange retires from football
- Tommy and Jimmy Dorsey become popular
- Benny Goodman organizes a band
- "The Lux Radio Theater," "Hollywood Hotel" with Louella Parsons, "Buck Rogers in the Twenty-fifth Century," "Bobby Benson," "Jack Armstrong, the All-American Boy"—radio

Name the Year
194__

In the News
- U.S. Department of Defense
- U.S. Air Force
- The Marshall Plan
- Blacks in major league baseball—Jackie Robinson joins the Brooklyn Dodgers
- Dead Sea Scrolls discovered
- Thor Heyerdahl sails on balsa raft from Peru to Polynesia

New Products, Fads, and Fashion
- Polaroid cameras
- Jukeboxes
- "Bebop"
- "Howdy Doody"
- Christian Dior, full skirts below calf, bosoms and hips emphasized

Music, Sports, and Entertainment
- Songs—"Tenderly," "Almost Like Being in Love," "Old Devil Moon"
- Jack Kramer dominates tennis
- Babe Didrikson Zaharias wins British women's amateur golf championship
- Dizzy Gillespie and Charlie Parker become popular
- "Meet The Press" captures attention
- "You Bet Your Life," "America's Town Meeting of the Air," Fanny Brice as Baby Snooks—radio

- "The Kraft Theater," "Howdy Doody," "Roller Derby," Gorgeous George, Douglas Edwards—TV

Name the Year
195__

In the News
- U.S. Air Force Academy at Colorado Springs, Colorado
- Gamal Abdel Nasser becomes Premier of Egypt
- Racial segregation in public schools declared unconstitutional
- Joseph McCarthy investigations for Communists
- Commercial color television
- Academy Award presentations on TV

New Products, Fads, and Fashion
- *Sports Illustrated* magazine
- Cuban mambo dance craze
- Slim, snug-fitting, unbelted sheath dresses worn with boleros

Music, Sports, and Entertainment
- Songs—"Baubles, Bangles, and Beads," "Three Coins in the Fountain," "Mister Sandman"
- Roger Bannister breaks four-minute mile
- Babe Didrikson Zaharias wins Women's National Open after cancer surgery

- Arturo Toscanini retires from NBC Symphony Orchestra
- Birth of rock 'n' roll with Bill Haley's "Shake, Rattle, and Roll"
- "Tonight," "Lassie," "Walt Disney's Wonderful World of Color," "Blondie and Dagwood," "Your Show of Shows" with Sid Caesar and Imogene Coca—TV

Name the Year
196__

In the News
- "Cigarette smoking is dangerous to your health"
- U.S. bombs North Vietnam
- Edward H. White walks in opace
- Civil rights marches
- Watts riot in Los Angeles
- Student demonstrations against Vietnam War
- Northeast and Canada electrical blackout
- Ralph Nader becomes known

New Products, Fads, and Fashion
- Fertility drugs
- Body stockings
- Miniskirts
- Bell-bottom trousers

Music, Sports, and Entertainment
- Songs—"What the World Needs Now," "Mr. Tambourine Man," "Try to Remember," "Yesterday"

- 588 TV stations in U.S.
- "The Man From U.N.C.L.E." becomes popular
- "The King Family," "Dr. Kildare," "I Spy"— TV

30

A Laugh a Day
Keeps the Wrinkles Away

Patient: How can I live to be a hundred, Doctor?

Doctor: Give up cookies, cake, and ice cream. Stop eating red meat, potatoes, and bread. And no soft drinks.

Patient: And if I do that, I will live to be a hundred?

Doctor: Maybe not, but it will certainly seem like it.

✛

After a serious operation a lady was still in a coma. Her worried husband stood at the foot of her bed.

"Well," said the nurse reassuringly, "at least age is on her side."

"She's not so young," said the husband. "She's 45."

At this point the patient moved slightly, and quietly but firmly murmured, "44."

✛

Middle-aged woman: "My grandfather is 95 years old and every day he goes horseback riding—except during the month of July.

Middle-aged man: Why not during July?

Middle-aged woman: Because that is when the man who puts him on the horse goes on his vacation.

✛

He: Where are you going on your vacation?

Him: Yellowstone National Park.

He: Don't forget Old Faithful.

Him: She's going with me.

✛

An elderly clerk approached the personnel manager with some reluctance. "I suppose I'd better retire soon. My doctor tells me my hearing is going fast and I notice I don't hear what some of the customers say to me."

"Retire? Nonsense! I'll put you in the complaint department."

✛

A couple celebrated their wedding anniversary every year by taking the train to the country inn where they had spent their honeymoon, always returning home the same evening.

On their fiftieth trip they just missed the last train home by a few seconds. Forced to stay at the inn for the night, they were about to retire. Combing her silver hair, the elderly wife said to her husband, "There's summer in my heart and winter in my hair."

Replied the husband, "If you had spring in your feet we would never have missed that train."

✤

A reporter asked a man on his ninety-fifth birthday, "To what do you credit your long life?"

"Not sure yet," responded the old-timer. "My lawyer's negotiating with two breakfast cereal companies."

✤

Little boy: Did you hear about the 88-year-old man and the 79-year-old lady that got married last week?

Little girl: Did they throw rice at them?

Little boy: No, they threw vitamins.

✤

First old lady: I hope I look as good as you do when I'm your age.

Second old lady: You did.

✛

Old woman: We all march to a different drummer.

Old man: Not me—I march to my pace-maker.

✛

Q: What's the opposite of a friendly senior citizen?

A: An elderhostel.

✛

I used to be young once. What a memory!

✛

Pushing 40? She's clinging on to it for dear life!
—*Ivy Compton-Burnett*

✛

An old fellow fell in love with a lady and got down on his knees and said there were two things he would like to ask her. She replied, "Okay." He said, "Will you marry me?" She replied, "Yes," then asked what his second question was. "Will you help me up?"

✛

He finally invested in a hearing aid after becoming virtually deaf. It was one of those invisible hearing aids.

"Well, how do you like your new hearing aid?" asked his doctor.

"I like it great. I've heard sounds in the last few weeks that I didn't know existed."

"Well, how does your family like your hearing aid?"

"Oh, nobody in my family knows I have it yet. Am I having a great time! I've changed my will three times in the last two months!"

✜

Doctor: That pain in your leg is caused by old age.

Grandpa: Don't be silly—my other leg is the same age and it doesn't hurt at all.

✜

Reporter: So you are 100 years old. How have you managed to live so long?

Centenarian: Well, son, I got married when I was 21 and the missus and I made an agreement. We decided that, if we had arguments, the loser would take a long walk to get over being mad. And I suppose I have been benefited most by 79 years of fresh air.

✜

A fly was walking with her daughter on the head of a middle-aged man who was very bald.

"How things have changed, my dear," she said. "When I was your age, this was only a footpath."

✛

Overheard in the clubhouse of a retirement village: "It's not that I cheat," the golfer explained, "it's just that I play golf for my health and a low score makes me feel better!"

✛

An elderly woman was telling her daughter about a date with a 90-year-old man. "Would you believe I had to slap his face three times?"

"Do you mean," the daughter asked in disgust, "that old man got fresh with you?"

"Oh, no!" her mother explained. "I had to keep slapping his face to keep him awake."

✛

75-year-old man: When I die I hope it is in a hurry. I'd be satisfied to die in the crash of a speeding car.

85-year-old man: I think it would be better to die in a plane crash.

95-year-old man: I've got a better idea than either of you. I'd rather die from smoke inhalation from blowing out 100 candles on my birthday cake.

✛

Late in her life, actress Ethel Barrymore invited a group of friends to celebrate her birthday with her. "Will there be a birthday cake?" one friend asked.

"Of course," she replied. "There will be plenty of cake for everyone."

"And candles?" another friend asked.

"No," replied Barrymore. "It will be a birthday party, not a torchlight procession.

✛

Old man: This new hearing aid is the best hearing aid there ever was! I couldn't hear this good even when I was a kid! I've never heard this good!"

Old woman: What kind is it?

Old man: A quarter till five.

✛

A woman who was obviously in her fifties had just moved to town and was visiting the local clinic for the first time. "I just need a complete checkup," she told the doctor.

Before the doctor sent her through the routine of the clinic, he asked her a number of questions for his permanent records.

"What symptoms do you have?" he asked.

"I'm not too well," she said. "I have pains in my wrists, and I don't sleep well because of a backache, and I seem to have a constant head cold, and I see spots in front of my eyes, and I have periodic headaches."

The doctor made a lot of notations on his chart and then said, "And how old are you?"

The woman tried to look demure and said, "32."

The doctor filled in her age as she gave it to him, but right beside it he added another symptom that the woman had not mentioned. He wrote, "Slight loss of memory."

✛

A woman walked up to a little old man rocking in a chair on his porch. "I couldn't help noticing how happy you look," she said. "What's your secret for a long, happy life?"

"I smoke three packs of cigarettes a day," he said. "I also drink a case of whiskey a week, eat fatty foods, and never exercise."

"That's amazing," the woman said. "How old are you?"

"Twenty-six," he said.

✛

"Do you mean to tell me your whole family was shocked and surprised when your 95-year-old uncle died?"

"That's right."

"But if he was 95 years old, why was everybody surprised?"

"Because his parachute didn't open."

✛

Wife: I don't think I look 35, do you?
Husband: No, I don't, but you used to.

✛

Two old-timers were chatting about things in general. "The world isn't fair," the first one said. "When I was a kid, I was taught to respect old people and to listen to their opinions and advice. Now that I'm old, everybody tells me that I should listen to the young people."

✛

Everyone at the nursing home had joined the special hospitalization plan except a fellow named Gaylord. Since the deal required 100 percent participation, the plan could not operate without Gaylord.

Everyone talked to him, pleaded with him, and pressured him, but nothing worked. He would not sign.

Finally one old boy, a former professional wrestler until he grew too old for it, came up to Gaylord and said, "Man, if you don't sign that hospitalization plan, I'll break every bone in your body, then reduce the bones to tooth-picks!" So Gaylord nodded, took out his pen, and signed the paper.

A bit later the home manager came to him and asked, "How come it took you so long to make up your mind?"

"I finally found somebody who could explain it to me."

✛

Wife: Will you still love me when I'm old and feeble?

Husband: Of course I do!

✛

Personnel manager: I see that your birthday is on the thirtieth of September. May I ask what year?

Woman: Every year.

✛

"I'm not happy about those pictures you took of me," said the woman to the photographer. "I don't think they do me justice."

"Madam," said the photographer, "I guess you want mercy, not justice."

✛

Two silver-haired, genteel females rumbled down the main street in their aged coupe, made an illegal turn, and ignored the traffic cop's efforts to stop them. Catching up with them, he demanded angrily, "Didn't you hear my whistle?"

The octogenarian at the wheel glanced at him coyly. "Yes, I did, Officer," she said, "but I never flirt when I'm driving."

"You win, lady!" answered the cop, grinning. "Drive on!"

✛

Every five years a photographer was hired to do an expensive portrait of a wealthy matron. All went well for several years. But on her sixtieth birthday she indignantly returned the proofs, claiming, "This picture is not nearly as good as the one you took five years ago."

Looking at the proofs for a few moments, the photographer sighed sadly, "Well, I'm not the man I was five years ago!"

✛

Two ladies were discussing the upcoming dance at the country club. "We're supposed to wear something that matches our husband's hair, so I'm wearing black," said Mrs. Ferreira.

"My," said Mrs. Achilles, "I had better not go."

✛

A trim-looking octogenarian was asked how he maintained his slim figure. "I get my exercise acting as a pallbearer for all my friends who exercise."

✛

Melba: Did you see how pleased Mrs. Popoff looked when I told her she didn't look a day older than her daughter?

Pam: I didn't notice. I was too busy watching the expression on her daughter's face.

✛

Saleslady: That's a delightful hat. It makes you look ten years younger.

Customer: Then I don't want it. I don't want to add ten years to my age every time I take off my hat.

✛

An over-eighty female friend of mine wrote me a letter recently. Here's a part of it:

"I've become a little older since I saw you last, and a few changes have come into my life since then. I've become quite a frivolous old gal. I'm seeing five gentlemen a day. As soon as I wake up, Will Power helps me get out of bed. Then I go see John. Then Charlie Horse comes along. When he is here, he takes a lot of my time and attention. When he leaves, Arthur Itis shows up and stays the rest of the day. He doesn't like to stay in one place, so he takes me from joint to joint. After such a busy day, I'm glad to go to bed with Ben Gay. What a life!"

Name-the-Year Quiz
Answers

Quiz No. 1
1923
1938
1940
1955
1961

Quiz No. 2
1928
1933
1946
1952
1967

Quiz No. 3
1920
1937
1943
1959
1964

Quiz No. 4
1926
1930
1949
1956
1960

Quiz No. 5
1924
1936
1948
1950
1969

Quiz No. 6
1929
1931
1944
1958
1962

Quiz No. 7
1921
1939
1941
1957
1968

Quiz No. 8
1927
1932
1945
1951
1966

Quiz No. 9
1922
1935
1942
1953
1963

Quiz No. 10
1925
1934
1947
1954
1965

Other Books by Bob Phillips

The All-New Clean Joke Book

*The Awesome Book
of Bible Trivia*

*The Awesome Book
of Heavenly Humor*

*Awesome Good Clean Jokes
for Kids*

*The Best of the Good
Clean Jokes*

Dude, Got Another Joke?

*Extremely Good Clean
Jokes for Kids*

*Fabulous & Funny
Clean Jokes for Kids*

*Good Clean Jokes to Drive
Your Parents Crazy*

How Can I Be Sure?

*How to Deal with
Annoying People*

Jammin' Jokes for Kids

*Laughter from
the Pearly Gates*

Over the Hill & On a Roll

*Over the Next Hill
& Still Rolling*

*Over the Top Clean Jokes
for Kids*

Slam Dunk Jokes for Kids

Squeaky Clean Jokes for Kids

*Super Cool Jokes
and Games for Kids*

*Super-Duper Good
Clean Jokes for Kids*

*A Tackle Box
of Fishing Funnies*

*The World's Greatest
Collection of Clean Jokes*

*The World's Greatest
Knock-Knock Jokes for Kids*

*The World's Greatest Wacky
One-Line Jokes*

For more information, send a self-addressed
stamped envelope to:

Family Services
P.O. Box 9363
Fresno, California 93702